M
i
x
Blessings
d

---

by Jacqueline Doherty

Inspirational reading to take you through the year,
for the 'good' times... the 'not so good' times
and the times in between.

First published 2009

ISBN No: 978-1-904726-22-7

Published by Verité CM Ltd

Cover design, typesetting and production management by
Verité CM Ltd, Worthing, West Sussex UK
+44 (0) 1903 241975

Inside illustrations by Jacqueline Doherty

Printed in England

INTRODUCTION

Thank you dear reader for picking up this book, for some reason known only to yourself, your heart and eyes are perhaps searching for some wit, some comfort, some truth, some balm, maybe something to soothe an aching heart.

I understand these feelings so much, I wish indeed that I didn't, but sorrow and sadness have been a part of my life over the past few years.

There is nothing that we can read or have said to us that can change our circumstances one iota! However, I know, with an absolute certainty, that items we read can alter our attitude to our circumstances greatly and give us hope, strength and the energy, to deal with whatever life throws at us, the GOOD and the BAD and the ugly times in between.

In assembling these pages it is my desire that whatever your situation, you would find

Peace in your heart, when your 'world' may be crumbling around you.

Strength to go that extra mile, when the next step even seems too far.

Hope… for the day and for the days to come.

Humour, to laugh out loud again.

Faith… for the journey.

Most of all dear reader, I wish you…

LOVE, it is only love that sees us through and it is only '*perfect Love that casts out all fear*'.

Jackie

x

1st JANUARY

As we enter a New Year, never knowing just what it may bring, then let us remember those famous lines by Minnie Haskins that inspire us to trust:

"And I said to the man who stood at the gate of the year, 'Give me a light that I may tread safely into the unknown.'

And he replied, 'Go out into the darkness and put your hand into the hand of God. That shall be to you better than light and safer than a known way.'"

2nd JANUARY

Did you hear the one about two speakers on their soap box at speakers corner?

A tramp… not noticing the debate between the Communist and the Christian… shuffled by tattered and torn, weary and worn. The suit had seen better days.

The Communist spotted him and seizing his opportunity pointed to him shouting 'Comrades! Communism will put a new suit on that man!' A small crowd cheered.

The Christian without hesitation, speaking from his heart added; 'Brothers! Christianity will put a new man in that suit.'

The crowd grew silent.

3rd JANUARY

'For the love of money is the root of all kinds of evil, from which some have strayed from the faith in their greediness.' 1 Timothy 6:10.

4th JANUARY

MONEY... MONEY... MONEY

Isn't it strange the way we worry? Over money, cars and things...
We dream of brand new furniture and the status having money brings.
But isn't it all wasted? An effort down the drain?
Perhaps we should consider how we could change our lives again.
...When we're born, we're born with nothing, not a stitch nor crock of gold.
When we die we may take nothing, leaving all to be kept or sold.
How much better to leave a memory, to be cherished in our place
And be remembered as a 'rich' man in understanding the human race.
We worry about having more than the people that we meet.
Why do we crave for lots of shoes when some people have no feet?
There's a riddle that I've heard of...
Asking who's the 'richest' example....
A millionaire... or... a man with seven daughters?
The answer is the latter for he knows that he has ample!!!
And don't we always want more? And buy more than we intend?
For it's true, I'm sure you will agree... the more you have... the more you spend.
To have health is surely better than to have money and be ill.
Or unhappy and discontented with destruction of goodwill.
Some may say and quite right... that we need the cash these days
And yes, I do agree with them for we live in inflationary ways.
Money can buy most things to bring one joy enough
For most things have their price... but money can't buy love.
Having money isn't a bad thing... don't misread what I write
For indeed it can bring happiness and change wrong things to right.
But let's face it most worries are for money, though not all, (I'm bound to add)
And most crimes are committed for money, thieving, mugging, so sad,
As long as we eat something does it really truly matter
If we have a T bone steak or humble fodder on our platter?
So, dear reader... if money doesn't matter as I bring this verse to end
Can you kindly give me some... and I'll always be your friend!!

Jackie Doherty 1982.

6th JANUARY

Many, many years ago, I read a short story about a certain Chinese Primrose which had beautiful red petals. The piece went on to say that when the very same primrose was grown in a warmer temperature the petals took on another colour and became a beautiful white. Although a tip for the green fingered among us, I can see a clear analogy in the story for life in general. When our own individual surroundings are compatible with our needs we 'grow' fit and able, accordingly, however, when 'grown' at a higher temperature (with love, compassion, forgiveness) we can become an even more beautiful person.

For those of us who can understand this analogy, then let us, whoever we are, wherever we are, whatever our circumstance, take responsibility for the 'atmosphere' around us…….. and let's TURN UP THE TEMPERATURE!

7th JANUARY

The festive season is almost at an end… You may be itching to get 'back to normal'. Stop for a moment today to consider someone you know who lives alone and make the time to telephone, visit or write a short letter to them. You will feel better and most certainly… you will make them feel better too!

8th JANUARY

'Kind words can be short and easy to speak, but their echoes are truly endless.' Mother Teresa

9th JANUARY

I love the story about the christening of a baby in January. Because of the New Year, the vicar waxed lyrical regarding what the baby's future could hold:

"Who knows what lays in store for this child, he may become anything he chooses." After listing many notable professions he added: "He may be a suitable role model for many other boys to follow…"

Turning to the proud but puzzled parents he asked: "What name do you give this babe?"

Quietly and with a flush on her cheeks the new mother answered "Mary Elizabeth!"

10th JANUARY

'God is our refuge and strength, a very present help in trouble.'
Psalm 46:1

11th JANUARY

During January many people think about Rabbie Burns and his poetry. This was addressed to the Lassies for a Burns Night Supper. It takes the theme of wondering what Burns himself would make of Lassies today.

THE LASSIES

Ah! Tis time to pay homage to the lassies.
      To the fairer sex round these tables tonight.
But let's not detract from the reason,
      that we gather in 'Tartan' a rare sight.
You may sit and bemoan the traditions,
      You may detest the neeps, tatties and 'brose.
You may hold no regard for the Haggis,
      even less for the Jock and his prose.
Yet because of a man who loved women.
      And because of a man who could write
We sit amid pipes and strange muttering,
      attempting a commemoration tonight
Three Hundred and more years ago.
      Lived a man, a Caledonian bard
Who loved many lassies in his thirty seven years.
      He found to love one was quite hard.
A singer, a writer, an affable chap,
      how would he view lassies today?
He fathered 'tis writ - fifteen children
      and back then there was no C S A.
Ah! But the lassies these days are quite different.
      Auld Robbie would turn in his grave
They don't want to stay home and have babies,
      they want to get out there and rave.

They want to join men in their exploits
and now go to war with the men
They've opened and stretched the borders,
how would they've coped way back then?
If only someone had told him,
when he penned the great song 'Auld lang syne'
That in three hundred years it would be on Top of the Pops
But with different words this time......
It's not our aim just to compare the two ages
To make judgement on what's wrong or what's right
I merely attempt somewhat boldly
...to celebrate ...Lassies ...tonight.
For above his writing or music or drinking,
his first love was always...a lass.
And of his many adorations
'twould make the thought of true love... an ass.
Therefore ...what is a young man to do?
Declare love 'as a red red rose...
Or protect his own self preservation?
The truth is today... heaven knows!
Do men want a lassie to adore him?
Or a lass who plays 'hard to get'
As he struggles betwixt love and loves' power,
he'll drown if he gets his feet wet.
So, 'tis sad on this peculiar evening,
to toast those... (excluding the pads...)
Who refuse to be treated as 'lassies',
who would rather be one of the lads!!!
And yet... may I endeavour at one last gesture
To toast those 'lassies' ...not like any others!!
Those 'lassies' who love so completely
Those lassies who bore us... Our Mothers.
All rise... Our mothers!!!!

Jackie Doherty 2000

12th JANUARY

Have you heard the one about the weary traveller in Ireland who was in need of an Inn for the night, believing himself to be in the right vicinity, he spotted an old man resting near a stile and asked the old man how far it was to the nearest inn. The man replied without hesitation 'to be sure, it's only a half mile down the road!'

After an arduous walk the man realised that he'd walked much more than half a mile, more like five miles.

The following day he spotted the same old man that he'd met the day before and quizzed him 'you said the inn was only half a mile away and it was almost five miles away.'

The old man grinned and agreed 'Sure I knew that well enough, but had I told you that, you'd never have made it!'

13th JANUARY

You may be passing through a difficult time in your life at the moment or know of someone close to you who is… remember this phrase from the Bible which is repeatedly written throughout… 'AND IT CAME TO PASS'.

We have to look beyond the difficult times, it is only when we pass through a dark time that we come to appreciate the light, the stars shine brightly continuously but we are only able to see them in the dark.

14th JANUARY.

A true story. When I was up all night once, praying and crying and writing a chapter for a previous book, I stopped and said to myself 'I have no strength to continue'. I rose from my dining room table, turned the computer off and took time to 'do' my daily Bible study with the help of an 'OUR DAILY BREAD' booklet. Half heartedly I opened the pages to the appropriate day and began to read; *'My grace is sufficient for you, for my strength is made perfect in weakness.'* 2 Corinthians 12:9 .

I skipped back to the reality of my problems with a new strength.

Unsurprisingly, I further wrote my next five thousand words with a new energy.

11

M
i
x
d

Blessings

15th JANUARY

'Man maketh manners... But manners maketh man.'
William of Wykeham 1324 - 1404.
The motto of Winchester College and New College Oxford.

16th JANUARY

Did you know that the cheapest time to ring your friends... is when they're out!

17th JANUARY

'If it is possible, as much as depends on you, live peaceably with all men.' Romans 12:18.

18th JANUARY

This was written for another Burns Night Celebration as 'Lassies' Response, it was written tongue in cheek!

MEN

When you're talking about men...as women do just now and then!
You will notice straightaway a thing or two...
It's a man's world there's no doubt, and they'll almost tell you 'owt
Just as long as they depend upon poor you!

They leave hairs all round the sink
And some severely take to drink
...the other vices I'm too nice to mention!
On time they like their lunch and suppers
And their morning toast and cuppas
Not caring 'bout your own poor thirst a quenchin'.

They hate you driving in their car...
Unless you drive them to the bar!
And then wish that you had rather stayed behind
They'll really shout and scald if you mention going bald
But then we know deep down that love is very blind.

12

It's not true, men don't make passes
At women wearing glasses
As they make a spectacle from time to time
And how they love their sport
It usurps their every thought
And to interrupt is almost certain crime!!!

Girls! Have you noticed since the wedding
How the old man's really spreading?
But of course he says the silly clothes have shrunk!
Well I'd like to just remind
That when they said that love is blind....
Did they mean that love was blind when one was drunk?

You may think I'm sounding bitter
As I complain and witter
But, you know we really all do love our men
For if we all just met tonight
And had the chance to put things right
CHANCES ARE WE'D DO THE SAME THING O'ER AGAIN!

Jackie Doherty

19th JANUARY

Did you hear the one about the three men, two were cowboys and the third, their friend, was a Sioux warrior chief. They were out one day from dawn until dusk, working their new horses. There had been no chance to break for lunch and now before sundown the two cowboys were complaining how hungry they were and bemoaning the fact that their camp was little over an hour away. The cowboys noticed how quiet the warrior was and they asked if he, too, was hungry.

'I no hungry' was the reply and he got back to finishing off his final chores.

Sixty six minutes later they rode into town, entered a canteen and all three ate heartily, but the warrior kept on eating until the cowboys could stand it no more!

'An hour ago you weren't hungry, but now you have eaten four full plates' they observed.

The warrior looked up nonchalantly 'Then' was not good time to be hungry – no food.'

13

20th JANUARY

Another favourite story of mine that I heard as a young woman was attributed to Ghandi but I am not sure if it is true:

As Ghandi boarded a train one day, one of his shoes slipped off and landed on the track. He couldn't retrieve it. To the amazement of his fellow travellers, Ghandi calmly took off his other shoe and threw it back along the track as the train began to move.

Asked by a man why he had done such a thing, Ghandi smiled.

"The poor man who finds the shoe lying on the track will now have a pair that he can use."

21st JANUARY

I heard a heart warming wonder some years ago about a young man who had sat every evening for three weeks, at his beloved brothers' bedside as he lay unwell.

One night it became apparent that the sick brother was dying, Arthur, the devoted brother grew tired and distressed, he was both unable to watch and unable to leave the room before the end had arrived. Wandering between the window and the door, he picked up a book and began reading its verses, written by Adelaide Ann Proctor and quite amazingly a few lines inspired a tune.

There and then the musician penned the composition of 'The Lost Chord'. Arthur in time, became, Sir Arthur Sullivan,

How strange that out of pain and sorrow and much heartbreak has come a well loved tune and song that has touched the lives of millions.

22nd JANUARY

'The marvellous richness of human experience would lose something of rewarding joy if there were no limitations to overcome. The hilltop hour would not be half so wonderful if there were no dark valleys to traverse.'
Hellen Keller

23rd JANUARY

Down there, so the joke goes, below, in the underworld, the Devil was boasting to one of his newest recruits about some of the tricks he used. He opened cupboard after cupboard. The bottles were all filled with temptation after temptation. Each was labelled. Some were marked with different names Pride, Greed, there were many others, there was every kind of temptation in his vast store.

'But' said the evil one. 'If all of those fail, There is one that rarely lets me down!' He pointed to the biggest bottle of all labelled DISAPPOINTMENT. 'One dose of that and most folk are ready for any temptation you could mention.'

Sadly, although a joke, it's true! At those times, for some people even their very faith is questioned.

24th JANUARY.

There are seven things that the Lord hates and cannot tolerate:

> 'A proud look,
> a lying tongue,
> hands that kill innocent people,
> a mind that thinks up wicked plans,
> feet that hurry off to do evil,
> a witness who tells one lie after another,
> and a man who stirs up trouble among friends.'

Proverbs 6:16-19. Good News Bible.

25th JANUARY.

A third and last reference to the great bard. Having always loved many of his poems, this was written following a true 'situation' that I found myself in one year, in my younger days. As you will read, it caused me to be mindful of something that Rabbie had written many hundreds of years earlier, his poem urges us to *'Have the gift to see ourselves as others see us'*... and whilst I didn't have headlice like the poor wee lass in church, my own embarrassment was none the less painful... read on!!

Mixed Blessings

THE GIFT TO SEE OURSELVES

I'd often laughed, and loudly
At Rabbie's wee adaptation
About the lass, in church dressed smartly
Unaware of louse infestation.

A paradox of learning...
Those famous lines he wrote
A chance to see the fool in us
"O we ha the gift to see"...unquote!

But there she walked, head held high
An air of indignation
Toe nails polished, jewellery in place
An uncertain connotation.

Yes, there she strolled with poignant poise
A smile now for all who passed
Dress well laundered, chic and smart
A sight quite unsurpassed.

Hair gleaming, eyes bright, flashing teeth
A sight to turn your head
A spring in her step now developing
A confidence abounding - inbred.

If only... if only she had that 'gift' now!
About which Rabbie Burns had spoken
She'd slither down the nearest drain
Her heart would be so broken.

For yes! She does make heads turn!
And true she makes one wish to glance
But sadly and... hysterically...
Her dress is tucked up in her pants!!

Jackie Doherty 1989

26th JANUARY

27th JANUARY

Outside Salisbury Cathedral stands a sculpture by Elisabeth Frinck, it is called 'The Walking Madonna'.

Over the years I have seen it many times.

Last year, I was being photographed around this beautiful cathedral by a broadsheet photographer and my mind was drawn to the image of the fine sculpture. I was reminded how this gaunt figure of Mary strides out significantly away from the cathedral, the movement inferring a body leaning forward full of vigour and purpose.

17

How easy it would have been for Mary to have clung to the past and hung on to her memories of her son's birth. We can understand her pain in having to watch her son die, paralysed by fear and horror and utter sorrow, perhaps she thought like I have often, 'that it all could have been so different' the 'if only' scenario that would keep us in despair. During that filming my tears dropped unnoticed by the charming young photographer, who would have been unaware of my sorrow or of ' The walking Madonna', as I too, sought to emulate Mary, to stride out with faith in God, to trust in Him for whatever lay ahead, going forward to the life to which God beckons.

28th JANUARY.

I went outside to find a friend and could not find one there...

I went outside to be a friend... and friends were everywhere.

29th JANUARY.

It was reported in a newspaper of the late anthropologist: Albert Schweitzer,

"In case my life should end with the cannibals, I hope they will write upon my tombstone, 'We have eaten Dr Schweitzer. He was good to the end.'"

30th JANUARY.

It is reported allegedly, that when Mr and Mrs Henry Ford celebrated their Golden Wedding Anniversary, a reporter asked Henry: 'Sir, to what do you attribute your fifty years of married life?'

The reply from Mr Ford: 'The formula is the one I've used in making cars... stick to one model!'

31st JANUARY.

'What shall we then say to these things?

If God be for us, who can be against us?'

Romans 8:31.

FEBRUARY

1st February

Statistics tell us that by the end of January most people have given up their well intentioned New Year Resolutions.

M
i
x
Blessings
d

2nd February

I was particularly saddened when it became clear that 'WOOLLIES' was about to close! Now, they no longer exist in the United Kingdom! There are no Woolworths to be seen on the British high street!

The story of Franklin Winfield Woolworth born 1852 is a familiar tale for many who have been born 'poor'. Many view humble beginnings as a great disadvantage, however, I would disagree with that sentiment.

Young, shabby, Frank journeyed to New York in the hope of becoming a shopkeeper, but couldn't find a job. Eventually he was hired as a shop cleaner, washing floors, windows and the such earning a pittance. Frank had a dream and never lost sight of it, after many disappointments and setbacks, he eventually opened his own shop and became one of the wealthiest men in the United States of America. His surname became a household world.

Isn't it true to say that because he was 'so poor' it was an advantage in that he tried so hard and succeeded!

3rd February

BEFORE AND AFTER

I knew I had to lose some weight... when I couldn't close all my zips!
It hurt to think what I had to cut out... Sweets, creamy cakes and chips!

But why is it when on a diet you always want to eat?
You feel quite sorry for yourself and enjoy the unplanned treat!

Now I went on a diet before Christmas to lose some weight
(I'd always taken a moderate sized meal)... but now heap food on my plate!

But... what can a mortal do?
What else is there to say?
I know that I must cut down on food
I'm growing bigger and bigger each day!

No chips, nor bread, nor piles of spuds, no jam on scones with cream
No gateaux or cakes nor chocolate puds, I've got to reduce my beam.

I'm counting all my calories
Converting Kilojoules each day
It's when one's on a diet like this
That your friends begin to stray...

"Oh! Don't worry! Have another slice"
Or..."Of course you don't look fat!"
"What harm can another small piece make...
You'll waste away like that!"

And husbands don't help either! "You're fine the way you are"
But you know deep down you're s p r e a d i n g,
when you can't get in the car!

You catch sight in the mirror!! Does THAT shape belong to me?
Unbelievingly you glance again, then have a sweet hot cup of tea!

The kids all buy you chocolates, to cheer you up they say!
And while they think they're helping... it's temptation in your way.

THAT'S IT!! I'm coming right off the diet, for I just can't eat any MORE
For my troubles and endurance... I'm a stone HEAVIER than before!

Jackie Doherty.

4th February

'Fail to prepare and you prepare to fail.'

5th February

Are you familiar with the beautiful hymn *'O love that wilt not let me go'* ?

It truly is one of my very favourite hymns which I often sing, usually when things are not going as well as they could! It is a reminder to me that God loves me more than I could ever really know. The words are haunting and touch my heart each time I sing them and I am so grateful to the person who wrote them. It's rather an old fashioned hymn by today's standards and the tune definitely wouldn't appeal to most younger Christians, but I challenge

21

anyone to read or sing the words and not be moved. The words were penned by Dr George Matheson, born 1842, the famous Scottish blind preacher. It is written that his true love had spurned him when she discovered that he was going blind. Apparently his sister then devoted herself to looking after him, he had a huge ministry and was a gifted preacher attracting congregations of up to 1,500 each week, he had several degrees and achieved much in spite of his loss of sight at the age of eighteen.

The story goes on to say that the hymn was written very quickly on the eve of his sister's wedding when he was alone and there is speculation that suggests he wrote it perhaps as he considered that his sister would no longer be able to care for him as consistently as she had done. There is no written evidence to support this. One thing is certain, however, 'something' so wonderful, inspired him that night, to write down the words that have brought great joy, comfort and hope to thousands like myself.

6th February

The Health Visitor was very impressed with the little girl sat in front of her, at six years old she was as proud as punch of her new baby brother and was involving herself in many aspects of the care of the baby, she listened intently as her mummy offloaded to the visiting official regarding the lack of sleep the family were suffering due to the newest member of the family!

At a suitable pause in the conversation, the knowing six year old butted in, that mummy had it all wrong and suggested that mummy should listen to grandma, who'd told mummy, only yesterday, to let the baby settle in to his own routine. Both adults were amazed at this and looked at the young oracle while she continued...

"After all, mummy." She offered, "You've made a mess of my routine! You put me to bed when I'm not tired and wake me up when I am!"

7th February

'Weeping may endure for a night, but joy comes in the morning.'
Psalm 30:5.

8th February

A NEWSCASTER'S NEW YEAR'S RESOLUTION

I'm only a poor old Newscaster,
Whose job is exceedingly sad
It depresses me so just to read it!
For it's growing increasingly bad.

I sit in your homes every evening
Trying hard not to express my own views
It depresses, deflates and upsets me
…this 'gossip' they've labelled as news.

I'm tired of political backbiting
Who cares who's divorcing who?
It's all sex, murder, power and fighting
And it's my job to read this to you!

I'd like to invent a few headlines
To bring Peace, Hope and Love to your lives
Like…'People are out helping people'
And not dealing in dope or flick knives.

I'm not even sure that you notice
The bad news and the suffering anymore!
What's the difference between bad news and bad news?
It all becomes such a terrible bore!

I thought reading the News was prestigious
A position to admire and praise
And I've worked very hard to achieve this....
But now think about changing my ways.

I'm suffering from nerves and am 'upset'
I can't bear to read sorrow much more....
It's unfeeling, disturbing not NORMAL
For I led such a good life before!

So...
I'm leaving the news team this evening
And about it feel decidedly glad.
And the last bit of news that I read you...
Is that at last the newscaster's gone... MAD!!

Jackie Doherty.

9th February

WHY DID THE CHICKEN CROSS THE ROAD ?

TO GET TO THE OTHER SIDE!

10th February

'Discontentment... makes rich men poor.
Contentment makes poor men rich.'

11th February

What do you see, dear reader in the picture below?

Do you see AN OLD LADY or A YOUNG WOMAN ? OR can you see both?

Whatever you see... you are correct!!

Study the drawing for a few moments and you should be able to see both a young woman and an old lady! Amazing isn't it! It's a valuable aid in helping us to remember that we aren't always right and there is more than one way to view things... arguments... situations... people. Sometimes what we 'see' isn't the whole picture!

12th February

'A little explained
A little endured
A little forgiven
And... the quarrel is cured.'

C.H.Spurgeon.

13th February

I heard this joke many, many years ago and it is one of only a few that I can remember:

The forward thinking vicar was thrilled to have been asked to speak at the local girls school, by their headmistress, on Sex and Christianity. However, he wrote in his diary, for reasons known only to himself:

–9am: Speak at Girls' School on Sailing–

The day arrived, the talk was well received and a few days later the Headmistress rang the vicar to express her thanks. The vicar wasn't home and his wife answered the phone. The headmistress was singing the vicars praises, stressing that he had certainly given the girls something to think about, the talk had encouraged much debate!

The wife looked in the diary at the said date and replied " Thank you, I shall pass on your thanks, only I can't imagine what he knows about the subject! He's only done it twice, the first time he was sick and the second time his hat blew off!"

14th February

Today is Valentines Day. All over the world Romance will be in the air! Sadly romance doesn't always last... True love is this:

'For God so loved the world that He gave His only begotten Son, that whosoever believeth in Him shall not perish but have eternal life.' John 3:16.

'If I speak in the tongues of men and of angels, but have not love, I am only a resounding gong or a clanging cymbal.

If I have the gift of prophecy and can fathom all mysteries and all knowledge and if I have a faith that can move mountains but have not love, I am nothing. If I give all I possess to the poor and surrender my body to the flames but have not love, I gain nothing.

Love is patient, love is kind, it does not envy, it does not boast, it is not proud.

It is not rude, it is not self-seeking, it is not easily angered, it keeps no record of wrongs. Love does not delight in evil but rejoices with the truth. It always protects, always trusts, always hopes, always perseveres.

Love never fails.' 1 Corinthians 13 v 1 - 8a. NIV

15th February

Did you ever hear the legend from Asia where there were two identical houses built for two identical families? Inside each house was a fabulous banquet table filled with all sorts of wonderful food.

The people inside however, could only eat with 5 foot long chop sticks!

In one house the people were pushing, shoving, arguing and fighting and poking people in the eye in their haste and greed as they tried to make space to feed themselves with the overly large chopsticks.

By comparison the other house was harmonious and everyone was enjoying the food happily, the difference being they used the overly large chopsticks to feed each other!

....

16th February

17th February

LENT

And what shall we give up for Lent?
Some material, luxurious, thing?
As we've done in the years that have passed,
yet this year begs for a different ring.

How easy to 'give up' the chocolate,
how impersonal to 'give up' one's diet
When He calls us - we 'give up' ourselves
and this year I encourage we try it!

It's the most personal act of submitting,
the last word in our spiritual life.
To 'give up' ourselves as did Jesus,
even when we have troubles and strife.

We can give up desires of the flesh
and boast about what we've abstained
But never can we boast of humility,
because then we just lose what we've gained.

As we reflect on what our Lord gave up,
then meat, coffee, milk seems too weak!
And the call of the cross beckons deeper
to give all we can so to speak!

So this Lent means a special abstaining,
required not for man nor his means
But a personal stride for my maker,
as my being on Him, totally leans.

It's a private, imperfect, abstaining,
causing more pain than a tum rumbling on
Yet, in the wilderness, alone in our searching,
we've His word to lean hard upon.

Yes! This Lent will be harder, I'm certain,
will be different in so many ways
And I'll pray that my flesh can be stronger
and obey all He teaches, all He says.

And when I am tempted to fall,
when my eyes look spiritually down
I'll pray hard to look to my Saviour
and suffer the cross for the crown.

No, I'm not giving much up this Lent,
I'll have coffee, sweets, biscuits and tea
Just surrendering all that I have that is mine,
'giving up' I, myself, me, me... and me

Jackie Doherty.

18th February

I have always loved the thought of being able to read and speak in Latin, at school I studied French, German and Spanish, and at church, Latin words often came up in the service and were written widely in the literature, later on during my nurse training Latin words were the norm for many aspects of patient care and it has always held an attraction for me but I am no Latin scholar! Whilst writing a book recently, where I wanted to use a small amount of Latin, the editor clearly couldn't understand why I insisted on writing those few lines in a 'dead language.'

For my part, I didn't really understand either! I only knew that I had to use them!

Following publication, how heartened I was to receive letters from readers who 'just wanted to thank me for using the Latin phrases.' Explaining that the words had meant so much.

Almost 2,000 years ago Lucius Annaeus Seneca the statesman and philosopher penned *'Si vis amari, ama.'* Wise, powerful words. Nothing dead about the language. It transcends time and translates: *'If you wish to be loved, love.'*

19th February

'It is well with my soul'

Last year, I was fortunate to attend one of Nancy Goudie's Spiritual Health Weekends held in Bristol, where approximately 500 plus women gathered to worship and praise God. These weekends are held each year and more information can be found regarding this if you are interested, by googling 'ngm' (new generation music). The whole weekend is a wonderful experience and it would take a month or longer to share it all with you... but as we moved into a time of music worship by some very young Christian boys and girls I was deeply moved to hear an old hymn given new life by a gifted young man called Ikay. Only the previous week at a Sunday evening meeting in my usual place of worship had it been played by Les, a much older man, than Ikay, in our congregation. Even as I had sung it then it had touched me deeply, as before we had begun to sing the old hymn, Les had explained just how the song had come to be written.

Horatio Spafford born in 1828 in New York, became a lawyer and was a deeply spiritual Presbyterian. He suffered much grief in his life beginning with a fire in Chicago and the loss of a son. Two years later he arranged a trip to Europe for himself, his wife and their four daughters. At the last minute due to a business meeting he wasn't able to travel with his family, they left on the s.s. Ville du Havre which was struck by an English vessel. The survivors were eventually landed in Cardiff, Wales and Horatio received a telegram from his wife saying 'saved alone.' His four daughters had died.

He travelled over to join his wife and it is said at the point of crossing where his daughters had drowned he wrote the haunting words of 'It is well with my soul.'

For non-believers it is hard to understand how a man who has suffered such great losses can write *'...it is well with my soul'*.

Within a space of a few days I had sung this song in worship led by an older man and then led by a younger man. The song written in 1873 or 74 crosses time, crosses age, crosses continents. No matter what troubles come our way... and we know that trouble comes! (I have learned in my own life that trouble never comes alone!). We would do well to sing this hymn and lay it all down at the foot of the cross. We too then will be able to sing and more importantly mean and understand the words:

'When peace like a river, attendeth my soul
When sorrows like sea billows roll;
Whatever my lot, Thou has taught me to say
It is well, it is well with my soul.'

20th February

I love the story about the Scottish minister who was very popular with the kirk he pastored but not so, his young wife. She loved to wear the latest Paris fashions and was the talk of the small town where they lived for being materialistic and frivolous!

The newly wed minister aware of the talk surrounding his wife and her numerous new clothes decided to have a talk with her about it, at a suitable moment he broached the subject:

"The townsfolk are talking about all your new clothes." He began, and ended in saying " Next time you're tempted to buy a new outfit, show restraint, if that fails quote scripture and say 'Get thee behind me, Satan!' that should work.

Hoping that would be the end of it, he resolved never to mention it again.

However, the very next Sunday, there she was in the kirk, wearing a most beautiful outfit, the likes of which had never been seen in the whole of Scotland, never mind the small town in which they lived. Everyone looked at her, indeed they couldn't help it, she looked like a mannequin from head to toe.

After the service the minister was apoplectic! Had she not listened to him?

"Did you not hear what I said about resisting temptation? Did I not say to quote scripture?"

"Oh, yes dear, I heard what you told me. I thought I would just try the outfit on and see what it looked like, I was looking in the mirror and was tempted, when I pleaded 'Get thee behind me' a voice came to me saying 'och! Mary it looks even better from behind !'"

31

21st February

'So, if you think you are standing firm, be careful that you don't fall! No temptation has seized you except what is common to man. And God is faithful, He will not let you be tempted beyond what you can bear. But when you are tempted, he will also provide a way out so you can stand up under it.' 1 Corinthians 10:12,13.

22nd February

LOVE... OVER LAW

Do you listen like I to the news?
Are you shocked any more by their tales?
Do you sit there unemotionally listening?
Do you care why our care system fails?

Have you heard about crimes in our cities?
Have you read there's no room in our jails?
What's happened? Will man never change?
Are we doomed to run right off the rails?

Looking back this is nothing that's new,
poor old Moses had a job on his hands
God gave him the commandments for living,
these laws now in all lands still stand.

And still man cannot stop sinning,
by the laws he will always fall short
On his own he's lost before starting,
please listen while I just share a thought!

When Jesus came and was questioned
about which was the greatest commandment
He answered with insight and wisdom...
While some had (and sadly still have) total
misunderstandment!

He came not to abolish the law,
but to make their teachings come true
Jesus said this in Matthew's account,
but is this gobbledygook to you?

To keep the commandments is a good thing,
but Jesus gave us a staggering word
About which of them all was the greatest,
I'll tell you in case you've not heard...

He said,...'the greatest of all was to love God
With all our hearts, all our souls and our mind'
And secondly, now this one's much harder
And calls for love of a much deeper kind.

And it's this one that causes us problems...
LOVE YOUR NEIGHBOUR AS YOURSELF
Let's try not to kid one another,
we'd rather leave this one on the shelf.

And yet, if only we could keep these two 'greats',
we'd have no need of the rest
We'd have no need of the jail cells,
no putting the Law to the test.

It's so easy and yet very hard,
for neighbours can be so hard to love
The secret's not to rely on your own strength,
but on God's help in abundance from above.

And so... The world goes on in a sadness,
not knowing this power from above
Christians! Let's show and tell of the difference,
of this great power that is simply called LOVE.

Jackie Doherty.

23rd February

Christopher Wren was only 25 when he was appointed Professor of Astronomy at a London College.

In his late seventies he watched the last stone being laid at St Paul's Cathedral. The young Astronomer had become a great architect whose designs always looked heavenwards, he created domes, steeples, and towers, his early habit of looking upward, learnt as a young man seemingly never left him.

Whilst we may never be either an astronomer or an architect, we could take a leaf out of his book and we never know just what we too can achieve by looking up!

24th February

25th February

As someone who prays constantly and anywhere, I was quite amazed recently to read about an American astronaut who has prayed on the moon!

The story referred to Colonel James Irwin, who was on the Apollo 15 mission in 1971. Life hadn't always been easy for him, ten years previously as an American Air Force test pilot he was forced to make a crash landing from which he endured many injuries that saw an end to his flying days. In hospital he kept asking God why this had happened, eventually he came to terms with it and experienced a new faith in God which led to a full recovery and he was chosen to train as an astronaut.

He openly reported 'feeling' God's presence like never before when he walked on the moon, so much so that about a year later he devoted his life to serving God.

Not many of us, more likely none of us, will ever know what it is like to walk on the moon but we can truly experience God's presence anywhere and anytime.

··

26th February

'Lives of great men all remind us

We can make our lives sublime,

And departing, leave behind us

Footprints on the sands of time.'

Longfellow. A Psalm of life.

··

27th February

Did you hear the joke about the young, keen, policeman who took his job very seriously and had arrested almost everyone in the small Welsh village or warned them of a misdemeanour, all except the local priest that is … he just couldn't catch him doing anything wrong at all … ever! This made him all the more determined and the policeman began to watch him closely and lo and behold, whilst he was following the priest one day on his bicycle it seemed that he almost wasn't going to stop in time for a red light, but at the

M
i
x
Blessings
d

last minute the priest was able to stop in time. In desperation the young policeman blurted out: "Bah! Nearly had you that time father!"

To which the chuckling priest responded: Aye, and you'll not catch me my son, God is with me!"

Delighted the young cop beamed:

"Got yer finally. Two on a bike!!"

28th February

'The Lord is near to all who call on Him, to all who call on Him in truth.' Psalm 145:18.

MARCH

1st March

St David's Day

LOSING A FRIEND

I'm losing a good friend quite shortly
Who'll be 'off' to heaven knows where!
And life will roll on in the absence
But don't think that I don't give a care!

For I'm sorry to see this friend leave me
We've had some good times on the way
All good things must end, I've been told
So Goodbye we will finally say.

It's hard to express what I'm feeling
Are you aware? Do my feelings you know?
The plans are made there is no retracting
We both know that you do have to go.

You've weathered my idiosyncracies
And remained a very close friend
But life is so very temporary
We knew we must part in the end!

...And so without tears or ill feeling
We part for our separate ways
I won't turn around but do wonder
Which of us... will see better days?

I've just lost a friend that I'm missing
Who'll cheer me now when the nasty winds blow?
Perhaps I should've made 'some arrangement'
Instead of just letting it go.

It may seem that I'm being quite silly
And that there'll be a new friend along soon
But I'm not the type of a person
To change friends with every new moon!

I have to admit to a sadness...
...A lump that I feel in my throat
I've just lost a friend that I'm missing
...For my friend was my old WINTER COAT!!

Jackie Doherty

2nd March

March heralds in, a promise of Spring, buds are showing on trees, bulbs are pushing through the hard ground, there's an unspoken air of hopefulness, of regeneration, of new life. No matter how long or how dark the winter has been. March never fails to usher in new light, literally, in the stretching out of the days in the form of lighter mornings and longer days. If your diary is like mine it will give the times of sunrise and sunset for each day, I find this fascinating and am in complete awe of the seasons.

Indeed time itself has always intrigued me. Ecclesiastes 3:1 - 8 begins:

'THERE IS A TIME FOR EVERYTHING
    a time to be born and a time to die,
    a time to plant and a time to uproot,
    a time to kill and a time to heal,
    a time to tear down and a time to build,
    a time to weep and a time to laugh,
    a time to mourn and a time to dance,
    a time to scatter stones and a time to gather them,
    a time to embrace and a time to refrain,

a time to search and a time to give up,
a time to keep and a time to throw away,
a time to tear and a time to mend,
a time to be silent and a time to speak,
a time to love and a time to hate,
a time for war and a time for peace.'

Words written so many centuries ago, yet they could have been written yesterday, the writer was initially searching for the meaning of life.

Many go through the same soul searching in their own lives and turn to many things to try and make their life meaningful: work, shopping, food, alcohol, drugs, sex, gambling, material gain, amongst other things. None of the above seem to fulfil the one seeking an answer to their soul searching. Countless thousands upon thousands of believers can testify that God alone and having a personal relationship with Jesus Christ and the Holy Spirit brings a real answer to any of the meaning of life questions.

For many, it is often during the 'dark' days of trouble that they find the meaning of life.

For those of you reading this who have troubles in your life, I hope you can take some comfort from the thought that, 'it is always darkest before the dawn."

··

3rd March

4th March

'Every man, for the sake of the great blessed Mother in Heaven, and for the love of his own little mother on earth, should handle all womankind gently and hold them in all honour.' Alfred Lord Tennyson.

5th March

It's only an analogy... but for me it is a very powerful one with a simple message. If you are struggling like many do with the idea of 'being transformed' as written about in 1 Corinthians 12:1-3, then let me remind you about the humble caterpillar. If we were able to speak to the caterpillar he would never... ever... believe us, when we told him that one day he would be transformed from his 'grubby' self into a most delicate and beautiful creature known as a butterfly! He would think you were off your rocker! Born to eat, eat, eat he would never dream that he would be a thing of beauty and of such use in God's creation! He would find it impossible to believe that he  would eventually, after enduring a long, slow and perhaps painful transformation break out of a chrysalis into something so breathtakingly beautiful.

Perhaps this is what Emily Dickinson 1830 - 1886, was hinting at in her poem *'My Cocoon Tightens, Colours Tease.'*

6th March

Hamish was away from his beloved Scotland and was very homesick indeed. He had little money but would call home each weekend with an update:

"Ay an how are the noisy neighbours the night, hen?" enquired his worried mother as Hamish kept telling her and all the kinfolk, how unfriendly and noisy the neighbours were, knocking on his wall all hours of the night! Making life unbearable for her wee Hamish with all their ballyhoo.

"I take no heed, ma... I just keep playing ma bagpipes!!"

7th March

'Listen, I tell you a mystery: We will not all sleep, but we will all be changed-in a flash, in the twinkling of an eye, at the last trumpet. For the trumpet will sound, the dead will be raised imperishable and we will be changed.' 1 Corinthians 15:51-52.

8th March

A ROUGH CROSSING… IT'S ENOUGH TO MAKE YOU SICK!

If you, like me, just recently, had occasion to travel the seas,
Then you may have laughed as I did at sickly people on bended knees.

For I'm a seasoned traveller! No pills or such to take
And from laughing at all those sickly folk, my poor old sides did ache!

I'm from a seaport city, well used to surf and tide
I found my sea legs young in life and have no jelly like inside.

I thought it so amusing, how they clutched their small brown packets
And some were not so lucky! Ruining unsuspecting jackets!

Soon I felt more sympathetic, the retching had made me uneasy
I felt a brash rise in my mouth, my tummy turning queezy

My legs just lost their standing and my flush was hot then cold!
And he who laughed last laughed the loudest… For I had no brown bag to hold!!

Jackie Doherty.

9th March

WHY DID THE CHICKEN CROSS THE PLAYGROUND?

TO GET TO THE OTHER SLIDE!!

41

M
i
x
Blessings
d

10th March

True story.

I don't know about you, but, I just love to sit in an airport and people watch.

All sorts of people come and go before my eyes, all nationalities, all shapes and all sizes. I often make up stories about who they are and where they are going. I have even been known to cry (often) when watching people departing and even arriving, as they are re-united with families or leaving them behind.

Quite often I am shocked and amazed at what some people wear to the airport! I often remark to myself 'I wonder what they were thinking when they put that on!!'

I say this tongue in cheek nowadays, knowing only too well on a personal level just how one can arrive at an airport looking dishevelled!!

Some years ago we were living in Germany and my husband was flying to UK very early one cold winter morning. He left home at 4.30 and was driven to the airport in provided transport. Once he'd set off I returned to bed and was awakened by the downstairs telephone ringing. It was 5.10a.m. and knowing that it could only mean trouble I jumped out of the bed and raced down the stairs, well... raced down some of the stairs... I fell down the rest... right to the bottom, I managed to drag myself to the phone and pick up the receiver. The voice on the other end begged in desperation:

"Jack, I've picked up the wrong passport... "

Interrupting and without hesitation I replied: "I'm on my way!"

Collecting the correct passport I threw on a poncho to cover my satiny (polyester) nightie, slipped on a pair of flipflops and limped to the car and then dashed to the airport.

Ten minutes or so down the Autobahn it occurred to me that I didn't actually know which airport my husband was at !! It could have been one of three!

I couldn't waste precious time in calling my hubby and more to the point he never carries his mobile as he dislikes mobile phones! Praying all the way, I was both thankful and relieved to discover I'd reached the correct airport !

I pulled over and parked in a drop off point, ran inside handed over the correct passport, kissed my hubby adieu for the second time that morning, caught sight of many people staring at me in disbelief, caught myself in the airport mirror and caught 'not a pretty sight!'

Middle of winter - crazy looking grey haired woman brandishing passport; hair completely unkempt; no lipstick; wearing poncho over nightwear; bare, badly bruised (from fall), stubbly legs with flip flops on the end.

The vision half scared me to death... not only from the embarrassment.

A lesson in the making!

I never now remark about the dress code of my fellow passengers... there but for the grace of God go I !!

11th March

'God moves in a mysterious way
His wonders to perform...'

There can't be many people who don't know these famous words but I wonder if many know who wrote them?

They were written by William Cowper 1731 - 1800.

Cowper was a famous hymn writer of his day but was equally a gifted poet. Sadly his mother died when he was six years old, his father was chaplain to George II. John Newton was his pastor and friend (his own mother had died when he was just six also).

Elizabeth Barrett Browning herself wrote a poem called *Cowper's Grave* in which she recognises some of the struggles he encountered in his life.

Cowper spent his lifetime fighting depression, insanity and suicidal thoughts. He often found solace and peace in reading his bible.

Much of what he experienced is set down in his writing, none more so than in the famous lines of *'O! FOR A CLOSER WALK WITH GOD.'*

12th March

'There is an enduring tenderness in the love of a mother to a son that transcends all other affections of the heart.

It is neither to be chilled by selfishness, nor daunted by danger, nor weakened by worthlessness, nor stifled by ingratitude. She will sacrifice every comfort to his convenience; she will surrender every pleasure to his enjoyment; she will glory in his fame and exalt in his prosperity; and if adversity overtake him, he will be the dearer to her by misfortune; and if disgrace settle upon his name, she will still love and cherish him; and if all the world beside cast him off, she will be all the world to him.'

Washington Irving.

13th March

Notice in church magazine:

18th July at 3pm the choir will meet outside in the church grounds for an open air recital – afterwards there will be a picnic. Bring a blanket to sit on and be prepared to sin .   !!

14th March

'A woman of noble character who can find?
She is worth far more than rubies.
Her husband has full confidence in her and lacks nothing of value.
She brings him good, not harm, all the days of her life.'

Proverbs 31:10-12.

15th March

COUNT YOUR BLESSINGS – YOU'RE RICHER THAN YOU THINK

I just wanted to tell of my blessings.
Of the ways that my heart feels and thinks
For the love of the Lord wraps around me,
far more valuable than any fine mink.

But do we always count our blessings?
With expression from deep in our heart
Or do we hurriedly say 'Thank God'
and on to other things then depart?

Are we sure of what a blessing is?
Can you tell what this word really says?
The dictionary serves to assure me,
it means different things in different ways.

Jesus spoke and taught the many crowds,
the Beatitudes, Matthew 5
And He speaks to each one of us,
if in our hearts we let Him thrive

The world regards a blessing...
as a pools win or as such!
The things I have money can't buy
and are worth a million times as much.

Money can't buy health or happiness,
or peace of mind or love
These blessings come from God alone,
our Father from above.

Wealth can buy the finest bed linen,
but never guiltless, restful sleep
Spiritual wealth comes FREELY GIVEN
and the heavenly bank account runs deep.

Do you worry about your clothing?
What new shoes you have to wear?
Be glad simply, for the blessing
that you have two feet down there!

The love of God and faith in Him
to supply all our daily needs
Brings a blessing of great deliverance
when we follow in faith where He leads.

Be grateful, give praise for His Word,
hunger and thirst for all that is good
For God's word alone assures us,
that we'll be satisfied... if not by the world... understood.

Feel blessed too in your trials,
for the testings you brave everyday
For these are blessings in disguise,
directing us on His righteous way.

For the gospel writers tell us,
they were tested over many long years
Each tribulation had taught them a lesson,
breaking down superficial and deep fears.

We scold and speak ill of our neighbours,
show no mercy or forgiveness of sin
Yet we expect such a great mercy of God,
when the bad deeds come from within.

If people speak badly about us,
laughing, scoffing, bringing hurt to our door
Remember Jesus who died and was innocent!
Suffer not from self pity no more!

What a blessing it is to have patience
when there's problems that could drive us mad.
And this blessing can be yours for the asking,
to not ask is so desperately sad.

I just wanted to tell of my blessings,
but they're so numbered there is no time to count!
The greatest of all is that God loves me,
my whole being from within and without.

Yes! I am truly blessed friends...
in my joys and my sorrows through
For I know that my Saviour loves me...
in my sin and my failings too.

Jackie Doherty

16th March

'Worry is like a rocking chair... It will give you something to do... But... it won't get you anywhere.'

17th March

I have often sung the song *'Amazing Grace'* without ever knowing the story behind those famous words! Written by John Newton, born 1725.

John's mother died when he was only six but she had had a deep faith and had taught him catechisms and portions of scripture, at six he apparently was reading Virgil in Latin!

Following his mother's death he had a troubled childhood, his father was a sea Captain and John too joined the Navy and was renowned as a very cruel man who profiteered from the slave trade. One night as a fierce storm raged a fellow officer said words along the lines of:

'It's because of you that we shall perish this night.' Newton replied, in effect, 'if that be the case then may God have mercy on my Soul'. As he went below deck he said to himself 'why did I say that, I don't believe in God.' From this experience Newton began to change. He left the slave trade and the sea and eventually entered into full time ministry. Newton went on to write many, many hymns including 'Amazing Grace' still being sung today in churches and on the football pitches! In later life he befriended William Wilberforce (whose own story of conversion is fascinating) and was instrumental in the passing of the abolition of slavery in this country. God had used a very cruel prosperous man from the slave trade to help destroy the slave trade. A God- incidence indeed.

18th March

BECAUSE SHE IS A MOTHER:
'She broke the bread into two fragments and gave them to the children, who ate with avidity.
"She hath kept none for herself," grumbled the Sergeant.
"Because she is not hungry," said a soldier.
"Because she is a mother," said the Sergeant.'

Victor Hugo.

47

19th March

'A man loves...
his sweetheart the most,
his wife the best,
but his mother the longest.'

Irish proverb.

20th March

A mother had her in-laws over for lunch.

She asked her daughter if she'd like to say grace.

The daughter asked what she should say.

The harassed mother said to just repeat what she had herself prayed at the breakfast table that very morning.

The daughter obediently bowed her head and put her hands together and began;

'Dear Lord, why have we got to have these people again for lunch?..'

OOPS!

21st March

'Likewise the tongue is a small part of the body, but it makes great boasts. Consider what a great forest is set on fire by a small spark. The tongue also is a fire, a world of evil among the parts of the body. It corrupts the whole person, sets the whole course of his life on fire, and is itself set on fire by hell.

All kinds of animals, birds, reptiles and creatures of the sea are being tamed and have been tamed by man, but no man can tame the tongue. It is a restless evil, full of deadly poison.

With the tongue we praise our Lord and Father, and with it we curse men, who have been made in God's likeness. Out of the same mouth come praising and cursing.' James 3: 5-10.

22nd March

MY MOTHER-IN-LAW'S TONGUE.

It's as long as any I've seen!
Makes you stare when once it's espied
It's so big–the size is enormous
and it's certainly not one you could hide!

It's edge is so sharp I'm quite wary.
In case it should just touch on me
As long as it leaves me alone,
I'm prepared to live and let be!

You may think perhaps I am cruel,
discussing a tongue in this way
It's a personal whim I'm expressing
and not for public discussion–you'd say.

The tongue's such a dangerous 'organ'
about which you can read in the Bible
It can get you into such trouble,
causing hurt and the odd case of libel!

It's strange I have thought very often,
how a tongue weighs less than a pound
Yet few people are able to hold it
and so gossip and slander abound.

But that's not the point I am making!
No, indeed, it's my ma-in-law's tongue
I wonder if it's always been that length?
I didn't know it when it was young.

It doesn't look healthy or natural,
more a sickly pale green I would say
And there's hairs growing right up the sides
(which can prickle if you get in the way).

49

M
i
x
Blessings
d

Now I love my mum-in-law dearly,
she's a friend and a good mum to me
But my ma-in-law's tongue is quite hostile,
not as peaceable as I feel it could be!

I invite you all round to inspect it
And then you'll all soon beg my pardon...
When you see it's as large as life itself
The tallest plant in our lovely front garden.

Jackie Doherty

....

23rd March

24th March

George Herbert 1593 - 1633, died at an early age and is famous to this day for his poems which have helped countless people make sense of their life, indeed William Cowper himself found much comfort from Herbert's works, some two centuries later!

Interestingly, it is reported that Herbert, shortly before his death sent his writings in particular *THE TEMPLE* to the then head of the Anglican community with a message:

'if he think it may turn advantage of any dejected poor soul, let it be made public; if not, let him burn it, for I and it are least of God's mercies.'

And it was published a few months after his death. He could never have known the insight, pleasure and comfort that his poetry would bring to people down the ages!

25th March

'All that I am or hope to be, I owe to my angel mother.' Abraham Lincoln.

26th March

'My mother was the making of me. She was so true and so sure of me, I felt that I had someone to live for - someone I must not disappoint. The memory of my mother will always be a blessing to me.' Thomas A Edison.

27th March

(Remember the clocks this weekend! Spring forward. Fall back.)

WHY DID THE CLOCKMAKER HIT THE CLOCK ?

BECAUSE THE CLOCK STRUCK FIRST!

28th March

'Wait on the Lord: be of good courage, and He shall strengthen thine heart: wait, I say, on the Lord.' Psalm 27:14.

51

M
i
x
Blessings
d

29th March

I don't know your circumstances, but as you have read through March you may have had a heavy heart from all the references to Mothers, it may be that you have a child away from the family home at present that is causing you to fret, you may well have a prodigal child, brother, sister, partner, husband or wife even.

You may even be a prodigal yourself!!

I know, only too well, what it's like to have a prodigal in the family and know what it's like to wait for the phone to ring with news, any news! This then is for anyone waiting for news of a loved one. Hang on in there and believe... that God is bringing the prodigals home!

THE CALL CAME.

The call came
Long expected
Sore awaited
Welcome... all the same.

Poignant sighing
Moments of caring
Seconds of sharing
Unspoken crying.

Then you were gone... into the night
So late it was almost morning
Now hope could come in...
As day began dawning

Back... to the waiting
Back... to the hoping
Back... to the praying
...Until the next call.

Jackie Doherty 2005.

52

30th March

An agricultural adviser spotted a peasant farmer laying in the shade under a tree and he noted he'd been there sometime.

Going over to him he asked 'why don't you work harder! Then you would grow more and could employ more staff!'

The farmer opened an eye and said 'Then what?'

The advisor sweating from the heat, wiped his brow and replied 'Then you could sit back and take it more easy!'

The farmer, obviously the wiser of the two quipped; 'That's what I'm doing now!!'

31st March

Probably best known for 'The Jungle Book', Rudyard Kipling 1865 - 1936 was a most magnificent writer, he was an author, poet, youngest recipient of the Nobel prize for literature and the first Englishman to receive such an honour!

Personally, I would find it hard to name a favourite Kipling poem as I love so many, but if I could only choose one, then it would have to be 'IF.' I have never been able to read it and not be moved in some way and often make reference to it. It is a poem I learned as a child and one that I read to my own children.

Kipling was a most copious of writers and he once allegedly said himself that the piece which caused him the most trouble was a poem that begins with the line: *'God of our fathers, known of old–'*

each verse ends: *'lest we forget- lest we forget!'*

In fact, he struggled so much with this poem that he threw it away, it was his wife who picked it out of a waste paper receptacle and sent it to the TIMES. The Times published it in 1897.

Kipling had a wonderful gift of writing and quite apart from the more popular items he is known for, are the wonderful works where he can enter into the person or situation that he is writing about, such as in Naaman's Song.

Mixed Blessings

Rudyard could never have known the pleasure his writing would bring to millions of people nor even to just one... me.

If you have never read his poem *'IF'* then I encourage you to do so today!

...Don't let it pass you by!

1st April

All Fool's Day.

A poor farmer and his son, were visiting family members in the next village which was a long way to walk so he took his donkey with him, as they reached the village the child was walking and the father rode the donkey;

He heard the villagers complain: 'How cruel for the boy!'

Some weeks later they visited the family again, this time the boy rode and the father walked, again he heard the villagers complain: 'What has this generation come to!.'

The following month the pair set off again, this time they both rode the donkey, on reaching the village they heard bitter complaining from the villagers: 'That's cruelty to animals!!'

Needing to make a further visit the poor farmer decided to appease the villagers and he and his son both walked leaving the donkey free and bare backed, to the farmer's amazement he heard the villagers say: 'Look at that crazy pair! Walking when they have a donkey!'

2nd April

To be Continued....

'Greater love has no one than this, than to lay down one's life for his friends.' John 15:13.

3rd April

Spring was in the air and a young agricultural student was home for the Easter holidays, walking around their large fruit garden he began to criticise the gardening methods his parents used:

"Mother, yours and dad's methods of cultivation are rather old fashioned, for instance, I'd be very surprised if you yielded more than six pounds of apples from that tree."

Surprised at his comments she replied: "Yes dear, so would I. It's a Cherry tree!"

4th April

'When the Sabbath was over, Mary Magdalene, Mary the mother of James, and Salome bought spices so that they might go to anoint Jesus' body. Very early on the first day of the week, just after sunrise, they were on their way to the tomb and asked each other, "who will roll the stone away from the entrance of the tomb?"

But when they looked up, they saw that the stone, which was very large, had been rolled away.

As they entered the tomb, they saw a young man dressed in a white robe sitting on the right side, and they were alarmed.

"Don't be alarmed," he said. "You are looking for Jesus the Nazarene, who was crucified. He has risen! He is not here. See the place where they laid him. But go, tell his disciples and Peter, 'He is going ahead of you into Galilee. There you will see him, just as he told you.'"

Trembling and bewildered, the women went out and fled from the tomb. They said nothing to anyone, because they were afraid.' Mark 16:1-8.

5th April

FORGIVENESS

> *Oh! How hard it is to forgive*
> *To relent and let bygones be gone*
> *It would seem that it's simpler to bear a grudge*
> *and to carry a wrong on and… on.*
>
> *To forgive is a fantastic asset*
> *To be able to say "please don't worry"*
> *For sometimes it can be harder for someone*
> *To be honest and say "I am sorry."*
>
> *To 'forgive and forget' is a saying*
> *- a cliché, that's bandied about*
> *But this can prove so hard a task*
> *- of which there is no doubt.*

It's quite hard to forget some wrongdoings,
and sometimes as hard to forgive
But if there's to be any harmony,
we must learn to love and let live.

And God, our father has taught us
to forgive whenever we can
His son, Jesus Christ made a request
'Forgive them' said He, meaning man.

To bring this to everyday living
To show that it's not being weak
We refer to another of his wise words
And...'turn the other cheek'

So friends, forgive all misgivings
Even when you've been done a great wrong
Forgive and forget all trespassers
And show that forgiveness is strong.

Jackie Doherty.

6th April

7th April

Many people today know the famous line:

'No man is an island.'

I often hear it quoted and if I could but remember the rest of the poem would love to quote it in it's entirety!

It was written by Sir John Donne 1572 -1631. Donne is one of my favourite writers and I would regard him a genius of his and our time! There is just so much to know about his life that it would take me weeks to relate it all and then I would probably do him an injustice, he was a magnificent poet held in high regard.

In 1615 he became a preacher, in 1621 he was appointed Dean of St Paul's Cathedral London and in 1625 He was Royal Chaplain to King Charles I. His sermons were very popular and used widely by other ministers.

He wrote, among other things, songs, sonnets, elegies, epigrams, sermons, satires, metempsychosis, marriage songs, letters, Holy sonnets.

In particular, his poems *'The Flea'* and *'A Patient Takes His Bed'* are just two fine examples of how he is able to reflect on a situation and bring the reader to full understanding of it:

From Devotions upon Emergent Occasions;

'No man is an island, entire of itself; every man is a piece of the continent, a part of the main.

If a clod be washed away by the sea, Europe is the less, as well as if a promontory were, as well as if a manor of thy friend's or of thine were:

Any man's death diminishes me, because I am involved in mankind, and therefore never send to know for whom the bell tolls; it tolls for thee.'

Words written almost four hundred years ago! John Donne could never have known just how often they would be used down the ages!

[Note: The title 'For whom the Bell Tolls' was used for one of Ernest Hemingway's famous Novels in 1940 and more recently it was the title of a Metallica song in 1985.]

8th April

There was once a young inexperienced minister who was trying to get a little sympathy from an older minister by telling him that he was worried he couldn't keep the congregation awake, never mind interested. The older of the men admitted that he too in the early days had the same experience but had found an answer to it, he advised that when it happens and he feels as though he's losing his audience say "I want you to know that I held another man's wife in my arms last night!" he promised that would soon waken them and to continue with "the lady was my mother!"

It didn't happen again until the summer, it was very hot and some were dozing, the children were playing around, and some women were talking, the minister remembered the advice and said very loudly, "I think you should know that I held another man's wife in my arms last night... " he could see all the staring inquisitive eyes looking at him, he had their attention, he attempted to carry on and said "... and that lady was... oh! I can't remember who she was."

9th April

'Not everything that can be counted counts and not everything that counts can be counted.' Albert Einstein.

10th April

The lack of forgiveness is evident in our society.

I believe very strongly in 'Forgiveness', it isn't that I find it easy to forgive because I don't, it's a hard thing to forgive someone who we feel has wronged us, if it was easy then there wouldn't be so much unforgiveness in the world, not just in the world, in our societies, our workplaces, our homes and more importantly in our hearts.

Over the years God has taught me much about forgiveness, almost on every level, just when I think I have learned all there is about this serious problem then wham! I learn something afresh, I have had to forgive people who weren't sorry for the hurt they have caused and certainly not repentant but in so doing, it has helped to keep my slate clean, so to speak, before God.

I have even had to ask forgiveness of people who didn't know that I was harbouring seeds of hate in my heart toward them, a very hard thing to do. One could reason with oneself that if they had no idea of how I had felt then why bother to bring it up at all? Let it be. In some circumstances, I can see it would be right to do this but mostly this is not God's way. He wants to clean up our hearts and to do so, is often painful and demands more of us than being comfortable. It demands our attention to detail in removing any thing which hinders our close walk with God our father.

Over five years ago, I was at a Ladies Fellowship meeting in Holland and the topic was 'forgiveness' and loving our enemies. I was comfortable with this subject, I could talk about the subject for ages, all was going well until the Holy Spirit challenged me about the seeds of hatred I was holding in my heart against a young man. I fell silent as others chatted in the group. What a hypocrite I was! I had in my heart blamed this young man for my own son taking drugs. (This is a common practise to blame others for things, rather than the individual- we live in a society were we love to blame people).

I didn't even know this young man at the time nor where he lived but I knew what I had to do. As soon as I got home I sat and wrote a long letter and asked this person to forgive me for feeling hatred toward him. I posted the letter knowing that probably he would laugh at me, that others may laugh at me, I had no idea how to get it to him and therefore sent it to someone that was once his music manager and asked him to pass it on. I knew that I absolutely had to do this if I was to feel right before God. To lay it at the foot of the cross. (this incident is well documented in my book *Pete Doherty, My Prodigal Son*)

As it turned out three weeks later this man received my letter and called me late into the night (early morning) and said it was the best letter he had ever received.

I understand what it feels like to feel forgiven! There's no greater feeling. I understand what it feels like to forgive. Both feelings are healthy, they're empowering and humbling at the same time.

I see and feel unforgiveness all around me, friends who can't forgive their family members for something that happened years before, wives who can't forgive husbands, men who can't forgive their children. Children who can't forgive their parents. It breaks my heart that they don't understand forgiveness even less practise it. It amazes me that they would rather live out their lives in a hurting hostile way than to seek peace and move on.

When one person chooses not to forgive, two people suffer as a result and often this spills over into more, into family feuds, into warring communities, into fighting nations.

Once when I was speaking at a prison on Love, Hope and Forgiveness a young man, a prisoner, kept heckling me, asking me questions, during a break he approached me and with tears in both eyes said pleadingly "How can God forgive me? I can't forgive myself!" I wanted to cry with him.

I hope I was able to make him understand that God longs to forgive us. We can never undo the past, we must live with the consequences of choices we make, but we can be forgiven, He will move us to a place where we can serve Him, love and reach out to others for His sake. God can use our wasted years.

We are not left alone relying on our own strength to forgive others, we have the help of God himself. He will help us become people who understand that we really have no choice when it comes to forgiving others. Jesus himself taught us to pray 'forgive us our trespasses as we forgive those who trespass against us'

How about you? Is there anyone you need to forgive? Is there anyone you need to ask forgiveness of? Have you estranged or broken relationships that are the result of something you said or did? At the heart of all conflict is a selfish heart, a proud heart. Did you know God hates a proud heart?

God himself forgives each and every one of us completely. Wow, isn't that amazing!

Is there someone you could reach out to today?

....

11th April

'Therefore if you are offering your gift at the altar and there remember that your brother has something against you, leave your gift there before the altar, and go your way. First be reconciled to your brother, and then come and offer your gift.' Matthew 5:23,24

12th April

A TOOTHBRUSH

What busy wife has not yet found more to this stick than brushing teeth
A life span of around three months? There's more than that! Read on beneath.

It's believed life BEGINS at three months, for the 'stick' in cleaning spheres
With fifty ways to use your toothbrush, lasting possibly for years.
After sitting in your bathroom, matching the latest colour scheme,
to throw the brush after twelve weeks, makes me almost want to scream!
They cost a pretty penny! In their many varied shades
There's a sort of class distinction, some types just don't make the grades.
There's nylon, hard and medium, children's types and oral 'B'
Electric ones, single tufted… oh! varied as varied can be!
A craftsman's only as good as his tools, an old adage we've all heard before
But a toothbrush is only as good as its' owner! (the dentists agree I'm quite sure.)
After twelve weeks of scrubbing your molars, the young brush's life's just begun
And I said that it has fifty uses, some argue there's a hundred and one!

Window frames a fastidious wife's obvious foe 'give up' and come clean in a trice
When attacked by an industrious stick with the corners and grooves looking nice.
They're great for the back of a loo seat (and I trust this won't make you blush)
Where the seat is attached to the bowl, and this makes for a healthier flush.
Some use them on cookers I've heard, reaching parts that soap pads can't touch
Some men have been known to pinch them for use on their motors and such.
Ideal for cleaning cane objects, for brassware where detail is fine
I did say that there were fifty uses but as yet have not listed nine!
For processors, food type they're really a must, cleaning graters and shredders like new
For shoes, handbags, spectacle rims, though gently, don't push the lens through!
For small stains and tap rims they're second to none and for artists provides new dimensions
It's valuable artwork for children and is worthy of having a mention.

Who knows what's in store for old brushes!
A second mouth brush shop! Big money
Just enquire from veteran housewives,
they'll tell you the idea ain't so funny

You ask them they'll own up quite proudly,
they've a collection of sticks fit for war!
As they aid and abet in contravening
The Trading Description for sure!

If those brush manufacturers only knew
How we use and abuse their wee stick
But it's such a hard story to swallow
That the thought would just make them sick!!

So before you throw out your old toothbrush
Just spare a moment of time
Think! Has it really lived up to it's fullest....
Don't cast it out in its' prime

Jackie Doherty.

13th April

WHY DID THE DOG CROSS THE ROAD?
BECAUSE IT WAS THE CHICKEN'S DAY OFF!

14th April

In the British Library there are writings of Aurelius Augustine who lived from 354 - 430. He was a man who lived during a time when it was dangerous to be a Christian. His mother Monica had a deep faith and prayed earnestly for her son, I believe over a period of twenty years or more.

Augustine was her prodigal son. She never gave up hope even when he joined the Manichaeans, a religious cult from Persia. He was very bright, heralded a genius by many but was living a hedonistic lifestyle as a pagan.

Through the conversion of Augustine, the course of Christian history was enhanced, he changed from a chaotic man to become a Bishop, a torch bearer for the light of the New Testament and eventually became a Saint.

There is so much in this story that I can hardly do it justice in one paragraph, but there is a lesson for each of us … those of us who are praying for loved ones, those of us who have been praying for years… remember every prayer is heard.

15th April

Did you hear the story about the seventy year old lady who volunteered to help in Sunday School? The vicar, thinking that she was too old for such a task declined her offer. She could have wallowed in self pity or been hurt by the rejection and although she was down hearted and disappointed walking home, she wasn't overwhelmed by it.

She felt that she had much to offer and eagerly took the opportunity, when it arose, to befriend her new neighbours and their young children.

It was around Easter when they moved in and she laid on an Easter egg hunt in her small backyard, she made tea and cakes and was amazed to learn that not one of the family knew the true story of Easter!! Sounds amazing but it's true, even in this day and age some people don't know why we give Easter eggs!!

Soon, the old lady was holding her own makeshift 'Sunday school' (though it was usually a Saturday!) as she relayed all the wonderful stories of the Bible to the children. It wasn't too long before the whole family came to faith, all from an old lady who was too old to help in Sunday school.

16th April

'Forty is the old age of youth. Fifty is the youth of old age.' Victor Hugo.

17th April

'The parachute, like the mind is of no use unless it is open.'

18th April

'I can do all things through Christ who strengthens me.' Philippians 4:13.

19th April

FORTY? NO! JUST THIRTY TEN

There's a lot to be said for being FORTY!
Though I can't think of a thing just right now
But they tell me my life will begin soon
Though at FORTY I can't just see how!

I'm tiring already by the week
Fatigued and malaised by the day
My neck's gone incredibly baggy
My veins like the spaghetti Motorway!

The bags beneath eyes have no elastic
They've been stretched to the far sublime
I've noticed my hair's more than greying
For these rewards I've committed no crime

nobody loves a fairy..... when she's forty!

Mother Nature sees fit to distort me
And the bunions are well on their way
The laugh lines so long I'm not laughing
And my eyes grow more blurry each day.

My dentist says my gums are receding
That's polite for I'm long in the tooth!!
Yet, they insist, life begins when your forty
I'm not certain they're telling the truth!

Yes! There's a lot to be said for being forty
Though for the moment I can't think just what...
I refer to my age as 'thirty ten'
Though it doesn't reduce it a lot!

I'm fighting the war of the bulges
With a waist to make two Brenner passes
But at least I can still hear... and clearly
(That's when I am wearing my glasses...)

But wait... what was it my spouse said?
What words did he mutter aloud?
Something about me being forty...
I knew that he'd make me feel proud!

Ah!
Yes! There's a lot to be said for being forty!
My age I will never now shirk
For my spouse gives his written permission...
I've an extra hour to complete my housework!

Jackie Doherty, written for 1993.

20th April

21st April

I just love to laugh out loud, don't you?... and I did laugh out loud when a friend told me about her latest shopping expedition!

She had been out looking for a wedding outfit and found the very thing she wanted, the price however was far more than she had budgeted for.

Being a good wife she tried to contact her husband and ask his advice, hoping he'd say the thing she wanted to hear! Unfortunately, she was unable to contact him and left a message explaining her dilemma, adding that the outfit was reduced from £450 to £225. She informed him she would not buy it until she heard from him and would call him again in an hour.

He was rushing between meetings and eventually sent her a text saying.

No price too high darling!

She bought the outfit and was trying it on when he arrived home. He quipped 'Why bother to ask me and then buy it anyway?' She sensed his displeasure.

She said she didn't understand because his text was very clear and she showed him his text message. They both fell about laughing because what he had meant to say was 'No, price too high, darling.'

A comma is such a tiny thing and yet its misuse or lack of it can alter the context of a sentence. Likewise in life it's the little things that can cause big problems, we know too that it's the little things that matter.

....

22nd April

John Milton, 1608 - 1674 is probably most famous for his wonderful epic work of 'Paradise Lost'. He was a very bright scholar and had both a successful and tragic life. Perhaps this is what enabled him to write in ways that reached the heart of his readers.

He went blind in 1652 and wrote a poem called: 'When I Consider How My Light Is Spent'.

He indeed is one of our great and popular poets. His words stand today as ever they did despite the time that has passed. He was a devout Christian and most of his work is Bible-based.

All of my schooldays were spent in singing one of his hymns which you too may recall (if you're of a certain age!)

'Let us with a Gladsome Mind
Praise the Lord for he is kind
For His mercies shall endure
Ever faithful ever sure.'

23rd April

St George's Day

'Pleasure in the job puts perfection in the work.' Aristotle.

24th April

Donald was very pleased with himself when his Sunday school teacher asked the class if anyone knew another name for God. His hand shot up.

"Yes, Donald what is another name that we can use for God."

"Miss, his name is Peter!" The teacher was astounded and asked why he had said that.

"Because when I hear mummy saying prayers she says 'Thanks Peter God'"

Before the teacher could take a breath to begin to explain Johnny had put his hand up.

"Miss, miss I know it, it's Harold, it's Harold"

The teacher blinked trying not to laugh and Johnny carried on

"When I says the Lord's Prayer I says, Our Father which art in Heaven, Harold be thy name... "

Out of the mouths of babes an' all that!!

25th April

'When you give to the needy, do not let your left hand know what your right hand is doing, so that your giving may be in secret. Then your father, who sees what is done in secret, will reward you.' Matthew 6:3,4.

26th April

WHAT NOT TO WRITE TO A FRIEND IN HOSPITAL

DEAR MORAG,
As you lay there... I just felt I had to write
I hope that all is well with you...
And they've fixed your vein-y plight.

If you're looking for some starting points to brighten the nurses day
Then do as you're told and keep tight lipped and don't get in their way!

If you need to use a bedpan
Then use it what the... well!!
Don't store it till a nurse appears say!
Just ring your little bell!

Now don't worry while you're in there... I'm sure the old man's fine...
Don't fret about the dishes... piled! Or the week old washing on the line!
Do you remember your white undies? Well, they're a lovely shade of pink
Yes! I believe he boiled your red dress (and I've heard he's on the drink!)

Now, I'm not one to gossip!.. there's more in life to do!
Just you enjoy the bed rest... At least while you're able to!

What does it matter... about the kiddies' hair, not being washed since you left home
You just lay there relaxing Morag... the poor chap hasn't found the comb.

He's setting trends in this place, with the kids from roundabout
They ALL want to dress like your brood... With odd shoes and socks when out!

But you mustn't be harsh upon him, for he's coping... fairly well
Between smoking, chatting, drinking... he's keeping down the smell.

So, what! He's spent the money! Big deal!.. You mustn't fret
I hear the odds were marvellous... It's just a shame he lost the bet!!!

No, I'm not one to gossip... and you know I'm meaning well!
So, you just lay there Morag and enjoy the peaceful spell...
For... you'll need all your energy, when you come home once more.....
For the washing and the ironing will meet you at the door!

Well! I hope this little letter has helped to cheer your day
You know I always like to help, in any little way!!!!

Jackie Doherty

27th April

28th April

I have just come off the telephone; how disheartening it can be some days to try and make contact with a person on the other end! When you eventually make a connection you are instructed by a voice telling you what options you can make, why is it that none of the options ever seem to match what I want? The days of a personal greeting on the other end are almost over!

How very different it is when we 'call' (pray/talk/listen, to God! No voice demands press option one for quick prayer, option two for forgiveness issues et cetera et cetera! You will never get a busy line on the prayer line to God, in fact God loves us to call Him day or night. He is always ready to hear our call and even tells us to call Him!

'CALL TO ME AND I WILL ANSWER YOU AND TELL YOU GREAT AND UNSEARCHABLE THINGS YOU DO NOT KNOW.' Jeremiah 33:3.

The God of Israel never sleeps nor slumbers it says in the Bible, so we can be assured we have His personal attention. Your call is important to Him.

....

29th April

I'd love to share a true story with you about something that happened to me a few years ago. Over the weeks we'd all been praying for one of the younger mums in our lovely ladies Christian fellowship meeting over in Germany on the military base where we lived. She was a beautiful, gifted, zany, young Christian woman with two beautiful children but was far away from home and family and at times she was struggling, not least because her eldest child, Joel, was autistic and needed twenty four seven attention most days. Often she struggled with lack of sleep and anxiety over Joel's future. It was always as I began to pray for her and her needs that I would be overcome and really prayed that someone, ANYONE would come along and lighten her load just a little. Weeks went by and the situation didn't change much for her and when in prayer for her some time later, I wondered why no one had stepped forward to help her... In the middle of praying one day, the Holy Spirit challenged me and suddenly I felt that I should offer my help!!

There began a weekly offer of help, it wasn't much, an hour or so a week. Giving that time helped me much more than it did anyone else I am sure. Often my own heart was breaking as I struggled with problems of my own, yet in helping another, it taught me that sometimes 'praying' for help for someone isn't enough, sometimes we have to be that help.

Where God sends He equips.

....

30th April

'Do unto others as you would have them do unto you.' Luke 6:31

MAY

1st May

An elderly aunt always keen to save money, was wondering if her vet had any special deals for pensioners. On her next visit she asked the vet:

"Do you give discounts for pensioners?"

"Of course, if your dog is over sixty five!" was his prompt reply.

2nd May

'When a man's ways are pleasing to the Lord, he makes even his enemies live at peace with him.' Proverbs 16:7

3rd May

WAKING AGAIN... TO A NIGHTMARE

> *Awoken again... to a nightmare*
> *A never ending torture*
> *That grips your heart and mind and soul*
> *And aches... and aches... and aches.*
>
> *Awoken again... in a nightmare*
> *That presses each aching thought*
> *Crippling senses, disabling actions*
> *Not reacting as one ought.*

Awoken again... no peace now
In dreams nor when awake
A feeling of desolation
That your very heart will break.

There is no pill to fix it
No cure to ease the pain
Awoken again... to the nightmare
Again... and... again... and again.

My child, my child, why hast thou forsaken yourself?

Jackie Doherty June 2004.

4th May

Over recent years I have met far too many mothers, fathers, sisters, brothers, wives, husbands, families, addicts themselves, who can share in the heartbreak that yesterday's poem conjures up for the reader.

It is often written that for every addict in the family there will be at least five people that suffer as a result. I always say with some experience, that the number could easily be tripled in most cases.

Addiction can take many forms though. Sadly, it isn't just alcohol or drugs, it can be many other things such as gambling, shopping, pornography, eating disorders, compulsive obsessive disorders, habitual lying or stealing, smoking to mention just a few.

Many people take part in some of the aforementioned and are able to live normal lives (whatever normal is!). But for others their dabbling quickly leads to addiction, leads to a point of having no control over their behaviour i.e. they have to smoke, eat, steal, drink, use drugs, etc. No one wakes up and says to themselves 'Hmm, I think I'll become an alcoholic today!'

I firmly believe that you cannot despise an addict more than they despise themselves. They no longer have the control.

As I penned the above poem in the early hours, I was strongly reminded of God's great love for each of us. If I could feel such pain for my child how much more was God hurting for his children? Not only for my child, but for me too! In crying out on paper as is often my way, I came to realise again, anew, afresh, many things, all falling, as it were into my heart and head at the same time. That we are never alone, that there is a purpose in the pain, that nothing is ever wasted with God, that eventually, in His time alone, He would use everything for the good. Scripture long forgotten would flood my mind, bringing comfort and hope.

If you are struggling with some 'nightmare' situation in your own life, whatever it might be, then bring it to God. He cares so much and longs for you to call to Him. You may be reading this and thinking like so many people that have told me 'it's okay for you! But I don't believe in God.' Then my answer to you would be what it always is, 'you may not yet believe in God, that doesn't matter… He believes in you!'

History and the stories of many famous people show that it is often in the very midst of a nightmare situation that we 'find' God. There isn't a single emotion we can feel that He doesn't understand. He never promised us an easy life, but He absolutely promises to be with us, through thick and thin.

5th May

'If your mouth wants to smile… let it! If it doesn't want to smile… make it!'

6th May

WHY DID THE TORTOISE CROSS THE ROAD?

TO GET TO THE SHELL STATION!

7th May

'Preach the Gospel everywhere you go and sometimes even use words.' St Francis of Assisi.

8th May

A person has to be a contortionist to get along these days!

First of all one is expected to keep his back to the wall and his ear to the ground, his shoulder to the wheel, his nose to the grindstone, all the while keeping a level head and both feet on the ground and at the same time keep his head in the clouds so that he can find the silver lining!

9th May

'When you pass through the waters,
    I will be with you;
And when you pass through the rivers,
    They will not sweep over you.
When you walk through the fire,
    You will not be burned;
The flames will not set you ablaze.'

Isaiah 43:2.

10th May

DETOX

This is a good day, long may it last
Clothing returned, plans have been hatched.

Tremors receding, cravings are few
Sweating and nausea lessening too.

There'll be tears before bedtime and some in the day
As feelings to run fight feelings to stay…

But the cavalry's here, it's mounted it's guard
It's stood to attention, tho' the battle'll be hard.

I'll call for God's angels to stand at his bed.
I'll summon God's Spirit to reclaim his head.

I'll plead to God's mercy for favour and grace
To bless him with wisdom, to return him full face.

Jackie Doherty June 2004.

76

11th May

Girl: Mummy, mummy, do you think pineapples are happy ?

Amused mum: Well I've never heard one complain!

....

12th May

Who hasn't heard the words of a prayer attributed to St Francis of Assisi?

Francis 1182 - 1226 was the son of a wealthy Italian family. He was reportedly handsome and well educated and well known for his lavish parties and living the high life. During a war between Assisi and Perugia he was captured and held prisoner for over a year, on his return he found no pleasure in his old lifestyle and before long was setting off for war again, this time against the Germans. The night before he left he had a dream about being in a great hall where all the armour was marked with a cross, in the dream he heard a voice saying 'these are for you and your soldiers.' When he awoke he was so excited and told family and friends that he was going to be a great Prince!

On his way to war he had another dream in which the same voice asked him 'Which is better - to serve the servant or to serve the Lord?'

He replied 'Of course to serve the Lord.' 'Then why do you make the servant your master?'

He immediately knew what this meant and left the expedition, determined to serve God. As he returned he saw people in a new way and began to care for poor and needy people, beggars and lepers. He saw in them, that they were God's children for whom Christ died. He gave away everything he owned. He served the sick and the poor and soon found others who felt the way he did.

Many times he 'heard' God speak to him and even though at first he wanted to live a life of prayer and solitude he knew there were others whom God was calling and eventually he founded a church order known today as the Franciscan Order (he also founded three others). Above all things Francis was always teaching that Christians must show themselves Christians by their love for one another, as Jesus had told them. His favourite festival was Christmas and it is widely known that he was the first to have a crib with a

77

baby, to help people realise that 'Love came down at Christmas.' He even asked the Emperor to make a special law that men should provide well for birds and beasts as well as the poor and needy.

In 1224 his Friars Minor Order arrived in England.

He died at the age of 44. Almost 800 years on his work continues.

Lord, make me an instrument of your Peace

where there is hatred, let me sow love

where there is injury, pardon

where there is doubt, faith

where there is despair, hope

where there is darkness, light

and where there is sadness, joy.

O Divine Master, grant that I may not

so much seek to be consoled as to console

to be understood as to understand, to be loved as to love.

For it is in giving that we receive

It is in pardoning that we are pardoned

and it is in dying that we are born to eternal life.

[Note: The song version is used widely these days and is the Royal British Legion Anthem and is usually used in their Remembrance Service at The Royal Albert Hall]

13th May

Every single day of our lives we are writing the story of our own lives by what we say and what we do, how we behave, how we interact with others.

Are we using the wealth of the Bible to help us?

A well read and understood Bible leads to a well lived life.

14th May

'The sermon is never over until it is done.' John Wesley.

15th May

Patient: Doctor, doctor no one ever listens to me!

Doctor: Next please!

....

16th May

THE TEN COMMANDMENTS

'You shall have no other Gods before me,
You shall not worship false idols.
You shall not take the name of the Lord in vain.
You shall keep the Sabbath day holy.
Honour your father and mother.
You shall not commit murder.
You shall not commit adultery.
You shall not steal.
You shall not bear false witness against your neighbour.
You shall not covet.'

Exodus 20:3-17.

....

17th May

BEAUTY

I don't possess the beauty of an Ursula Andress
I cannot claim great wisdom that could suitably impress

I cannot own to being rich and all that that entails
Nor may I boast a figure that doesn't strain the scales!

But, I can brag and loudly, of a man who died for me
He loved me so completely that they nailed Him to a tree.

He saw and sees a beauty… somewhere deep… within my soul
And sets about releasing it, to make my person whole.

It's not a beauty for the eyes, for we know that eyes deceive
It's for feeling and for knowing, when Jesus we receive.

Mixed Blessings

My wealth is quite immeasurable, that I cannot count it all
I feel blessed beyond presumption, not least in hearing Jesu's call.

I can see and hear and walk; I can laugh and cry and think
I can move and talk and love, and freely, spiritual waters drink.

I do possess the stars, I own the skies above
Mine are the oceans and the mounts, made by our Father's love.

I meet the King of kings each day, no matter how I feel
I've never seen Him with mine eyes but feel and know He's real.

Jackie Doherty.

18th May

Overheard whilst in a queue one day.

Two young women were discussing ways of saving money when one of them revealed that she didn't normally take the bus she usually ran behind it all the way to work and saved £1.60!

The other, obviously a bright spark quipped 'well run behind a taxi tomorrow and save yourself £8 !

19th May

To be a Pilgrim.

Who of us over a certain age have never sung this wonderful hymn?

He who would valiant be?
'Gainst all disaster
Let him in constancy
Follow the Master.
There's no discouragement
Shall make him once relent,
His first avowed intent
To be a pilgrim

Who of us haven't been encouraged by the last three lines:

I'll fear not what men say
I'll labour night and day
To be a pilgrim.'

Did you just sing it like I did? This hymn was adapted from Bunyan's own writings.

John Bunyan (1628 - 1688), was not a wealthy man. The son of a tinker who became a great English writer, a Puritanical theologian and Baptist preacher. Although he wrote many, many things, probably he is best known for his *'Pilgrim's Progress'*, written in two parts.

He wrote, that as a child he heard a voice say to him while he was playing 'Wilt thou leave thy sins and go to heaven or have thy sins and go to hell?' Shortly after this he began to study the Bible.

John didn't have an easy life at all, he was no stranger to conflict and was outspoken and often he would have disagreements with many people including the Quakers.

His first daughter was born blind and a few years later his wife died, he was in utter grief but that same year he began preaching with much popularity.

His notoriety grew and soon he was in trouble for preaching without a license and was imprisoned several times as a result, one time for twelve years! It is believed that he wrote his famous work while imprisoned.

On his release he was granted a license to preach under the new law. He had a meeting house built and joined a non conformist group and had a huge congregation of about 4,000 in the Bedford area.

Again in 1675 he was imprisoned and ironically it was the Quakers who played a part in his release.

'Pilgrim's Progress' was said to be the most popular book after the Bible.

He was an extraordinary man! He could never have known how God would use his words to reach down the centuries, He was heavily criticised over his work but it never deterred him.

20th May

I love the story of the sailor who grappled with sailing around the British Isles single handed.

It wasn't an easy journey and at one point his journey grew treacherous, so much so that the army came to his aid and told him to abandon his boat or he would drown, to which he replied 'I don't need any help, go away. My faith is in God'.

The army helicopter crew had no choice but to leave him.

Some time later in a similar situation the Coastguard came to his rescue and he again, was told to abandon ship or he would surely drown, to which he replied 'I have faith in God - go away.'

However, the weather grew worse and the Coastguard called out the Naval Reserve to assist, they let down a rope at great danger to themselves and ordered the lone sailor to abandon his vessel and climb the rope adding that unless he did so he would certainly drown, to which the stubborn sailor replied: 'Please go away and leave me alone, my faith is in God!'

Angry, the chopper pilot returned to base.

The sailor drowned.

Being a Christian the sailor goes to heaven and says to Saint Peter 'I must say I am disappointed I had absolute faith in God and He let me drown!'

'You're disappointed!' said Saint Peter 'God sent the Army, the Coastguard and the Navy and you still you wouldn't listen and went and got drowned!'"

21st May

'Failure is the opportunity to begin again, more intelligently.' Henry Ford.

22nd May

Experienced salesman to trainee salesman: 'Always remember in order to sell something to a woman:... tell her it's a bargain. In order to sell to a man: tell him it's deductible.'

23rd May

'Get wisdom, get understanding; do not forget my words or swerve from them.

Do not forsake wisdom, and she will protect you; love her, and she will watch over you. Wisdom is supreme; therefore get wisdom. Though it cost all you have, get understanding.' Proverbs4 v 5 - 7.

24th May

LAMENT OF A HAY FEVER SUFFERER

Oh dear! Can't someone help me...
My problem's so unfair!
For I just can't stop snee ee ee zing
When the pollen's in the air!

I've sneezed until I'm dizzy, using tissues by the score
I'm sick and tired of blowing my nose,it's blotchy... red... and sore.
I wonder when (if) release will come and give my nose some ease
Curing puffy eyes and itchy ears and my permanent loud sneeze!

I can't sit in the garden
And it's a pain to go for walks
My neighbour's given up on me
... for I'm sneezing as she talks!

When driving out just recently, reversing carefully....
I sneezed and quite unfortunately... reversed into a tree!!
Imagine what the old man said! As I handed out my pleas
Actually, I didn't hear just what he said... as I was in a sneeze!

So, from sneezing morn till night
I am weary... worn out too
But let me tell you this my friends...
it's... oh! oh! ATISHOO!!

Jackie Doherty

[Longest sneezing bout was that of Donna Griffiths, it started on Jan 13th and ended 27th July in 1981. Fastest sneeze recorded... 167Km/hour.]

25th May

An ageing priest who knew his hearing was going, asked his flock if they would kindly write their confessions on a slip of paper and pass them through the confessional.

All was going well until one day, the note said; two tins of tomatoes, half pound of butter, one brown loaf…

The priest handed it back and almost heard a person say. 'Mia culpa, I've left my confessions at the corner shop!'

26th May

What's the difference between a butcher and a light sleeper?

One weighs a steak and one stays awake!

27th May

I understand what it feels like to be criticised and in the past have taken great comfort in the following famous passage:

'It is not the critic who counts; not the man who points out how the strong man stumbles or where the doer of deeds could have done better. The credit

belongs to the man who is actually in the arena, whose face is marred by dust and sweat and blood, who strives valiantly, who errs and comes up short again and again, because there is no effort without error or shortcoming, but who knows the great enthusiasms, the great devotions, who spends himself for a worthy cause; who at the best, knows, in the end, the triumph of high achievement, and who, at the worst, if he fails, at least he failed while doing greatly, so that his place shall never be with those cold and timid souls who know neither victory nor defeat.'

Theodore Roosevelt. 1858 - 1919. From a speech at the Sorbonne, Paris April 23rd 1910. Roosevelt became the youngest ever president of the United States of America, to date.

He was born into a wealthy family and enjoyed a good education but knew of personal sorrow in his own life – not least having lost his wife, who died just two days after giving birth, on the same day, in the same house that his mother also died, some eleven hours earlier!

He was the 26th President, an avid writer and the first American Nobel Peace Prize winner.

His words have encouraged many people around the world.

28th May

'One word of encouragement can do more than a thousand criticisms.'

29th May

A customer in a restaurant was tiring of the poor service and tardiness of his meal, in desperation he asked the waiter when he arrived:

'Excuse me for asking, but how many people work here?'

The waiter replied; 'About half of them, Sir!'

30th May

'Therefore, there is now no condemnation for those who are in Christ Jesus.' Romans 8:1a.

31st May

REPLACED BY GOD'S HOLY SPIRIT

*I've been thinking about the Ascension of our Lord in those days long ago
And of how he fulfilled the old scriptures from start of his life here below.
His coming as described in Isaiah, God's covenant for us now to behold
His teachings are ours for obeying, and power given to make us so bold.*

*After death He appeared many times to many people creating no doubt
They'd to wait for the GIFT of His Father, the promise he'd told them about.
They were frightened, worried and feeble, how could they cope without Him?
It must have been faith that sustained them, as their future grew terribly dim.*

*Oh! Yes I'm sure they must have been saved a cliché that one likes to use,
But it struck me just now with gusto! Salvation's the tip of a very long fuse.
Salvation is oh! so important, it's the start of our walk with our Lord.
But sadly can be a non starter in spreading the gospel abroad.*

*'John the Baptist had baptised with water' said Jesus as he left them that day
'But the Gift that my Father has promised, will Baptise you in a Spiritual way.'
The Holy Spirit came and fell upon them, embraced them with power anew.
This Spirit's not just for those old days! It's for now, it's for me, it's for YOU.*

*If your lives lack the power of God, tho' of your salvation you're totally assured
Then take up the Gifts He offers, they're yours and their mine from our Lord.
We too can be frightened and feeble, to speak what our hearts feel within
We're afraid of letting our barriers down, of allowing the world to peek in.*

*Accept this free gift that God offers, watch all your fears then subside
A boldness, a power will transform you, in your heart His Spirit will abide.
As it did in the days of the Apostles who were changed so from mice into men
They then boldly witnessed as we should, for Jesus is coming... again.*

Jackie Doherty 1985.

JUNE

1st June

You don't need to see eye to eye to hold hands with one another

2nd June

A few years ago, a dear friend of mine called Trish, sent me a book that in many ways changed my life. You may have heard of this book dear reader, you may even have read it! At the present time it has sold more than 20 million copies worldwide!

Mixed Blessings

It's a book that promises to change your life and I must admit that I didn't think it would do anything of the sort, but how wrong I was and how grateful I am for the gift from my friend. I now, strongly commend the book to you and if, like me, you have already read it, then I commend that you read it again!

It's a study over 40 days and I would like to share with you just one small aspect of how it changed my life.

The book was written by Rick Warren, the founding Pastor of Saddleback Church in California, which is one of America's largest and best known churches.

In January 2009, at President Barack Obama's presidential inauguration I was amazed, astounded, thrilled to see and hear on my television screen, that the prayers offered were by Rick Warren, so much so that I started to cry!

The book of which I write is called *'THE PURPOSE DRIVEN LIFE'* which poses the question 'What on earth am I here for?'

Before reading this book I was probably the type of person that if you stood on my toe I would have apologised for my toe being in the way! A bit dramatic but you get my drift! I believed very much what Jesus says in Matthew 5 when he is speaking out, what we now call the Beatitudes. I refer in particular, to the verse *'Blessed are the Peacemakers, for they will be called sons of God.'* I had spent my life being a Peacemaker, or so I thought!! In fact, I had been a Peace lover! What a world of difference there is between the two! Jesus NEVER said, Blessed are the Peace lovers!

Often when we require Peace we compromise many things just for the Peace, this was probably true of me and may be true of you too! I have now learned that it is actually okay to not settle for Peace at any cost and that it is better to be honest and be able to say 'Well, actually, this is not how it is.' 'Actually, that is your opinion but it doesn't make it right.' Et cetera, et cetera.

There are a multiplicity of ways and circumstances that this can be used and each of us know our own situations best, for my part I would be honest and tell you that sometimes I slip back into old habits and have to remind myself of the difference between Peace making and Peace loving and that if we want Peace, true Peace then we have to prepare, sometimes, to do battle!

3rd June

It's an odd custom, but one I have used all my life, encouraged by my parents, I suppose, I in turn, have encouraged my own three children to continue in the custom of hand shaking. When I meet old friends they often remark on my old habit, because before I kiss them, I take their hand and shake it.

I believe the custom came about to show fellow travellers that you came in peace and had no weapon. When someone shakes my hand I'm able to feel welcomed (or not), encouragement, friendship, sympathy and much more, for my part it is a way of saying 'I come in Peace.'

4th June

'Peace I leave with you; my peace I give you.'. John 14:27

5th June

I love the story about two great men of our time who always had friendly banter between them; the story goes that George Bernard Shaw sent some tickets over to Sir Winston Churchill with a note saying: 'Enclosed two tickets for new play, bring a friend … if you have one!'

Apparently, Churchill sent a note back saying: 'How kind, I'm unable to make the first night, but can come to the second… if there is one!'

6th June

The Beatitudes
'Blessed are the poor in Spirit, for theirs is the kingdom of heaven.
Blessed are those who mourn, for they will be comforted.
Blessed are the meek, for they will inherit the earth.
Blessed are those who hunger and thirst for righteousness, for they will be filled.
Blessed are the merciful, for they will be shown mercy.
Blessed are the pure in heart, for they will see God.
Blessed are the peacemakers, for they will be called sons of God.
Blessed are those who are persecuted because of righteousness,

89

for theirs is the kingdom of heaven.

Blessed are you when people insult you, persecute you and falsely say all kinds of evil against you because of me.

Rejoice and be glad, because great is your reward in heaven, for in the same way they persecuted the prophets who were before you.'

Matthew 5:3-12.

··

7th June

About four years ago I was asked to take part in a wonderful Sunday morning radio programme with Aled Jones, the famous television and radio presenter. One of the producers had asked if I was able to write a short poem for the interview but stated that it could be no longer than 2 mins! The programme was about 'Faith in the Family.' This was the result.

FAITH IN THE FAMILY

There's a faith in my family… of the Christian kind
I'll speak of it openly… not embarrassed, don't mind.

Not ashamed to tell people… from whom I gain strength
… which gives me the Grace, to go the whole length.

I pray without ceasing, to Father, Spirit and Son.
The bottom line always, thy will Father, be done. Amen.

Jackie Doherty 24/10/06

··

8th June

WHY DID THE SNAIL CROSS THE ROAD?

TO PROVE THAT HE WASN'T A CHICKEN!!

9th June

The famous hymn, *'ABIDE WITH ME'*, is often used at Funerals and I certainly remember older members of the family having it sung, at their prior request at their funeral. Indeed my own mother said the same thing to me often in her latter years, because it was one of her very favourite hymns. It's also recorded as being King George V's favourite hymn. The words just seem to evoke such strong sentiments.

A man called Henry Lyte 1793 - 1847 wrote the hymn, he wrote it just before his death. He had a very troubled start to his early life being completely alone in the world at the age of nine. He was a bright scholar and had initially wanted to study medicine but went into the church to serve God.

He had a varied life and achieved great things and married happily.

Eventually, he became a Minister in Brixham where he stayed for twenty three years. He suffered ill health and died, it is reported, of tuberculosis, in Nice, France, while convalescing there.

He was a gifted writer and also wrote poetry, sermons, etc, another of his famous hymns is 'Praise my soul the King of heaven' which I think we sang at least once a week at school and then often again at church! I read one of his poems recently which made me cry, it is a reflection of his dear mother!

Although he wrote *'Abide with me'* through suffering and pain, near the end of his life, it has brought much inspiration and comfort to thousands of other people!

He could never have known at the time of writing just how poignant his words would be, how they would be sung and used for over 200 years!

10th June

We can't understand it... it's a mystery to us that often in life it's the heavy burdens people carry in the form of illness, poverty, tragedy, suffering and the like, that can, instead of pulling them down, in fact raise them up with faith and hope. An analogy of this mystery can be seen in kite flying. How often we see children with home made kites that have 'no weight' that just won't fly! However it seems that when a weight is added to the end of the string a wonderful thing happens and it soars.

11th June

Kindness... In words creates confidence

Kindness... In thinking creates profoundness

Kindness... In giving creates Love.

12th June

A solicitor's dog had wandered into the restaurant next door and before being spotted had eaten a whole leg of venison from the kitchen.

The owner went to the solicitor and asked 'If a dog steals a piece of meat from my restaurant, have I the right to demand payment from the dog's owner?'

'Absolutely,' the solicitor responded.

The restaurant owner handed him a bill for thirty pounds and sixty two pence, at which the solicitor never turned a hair and immediately wrote a cheque for the said amount.

Several days later the restaurant owner received a bill for £50 from the solicitor, which read 'Consultation Fees.' !

13th June

'The wisdom that comes from heaven is first of all pure; then peace-loving, considerate, submissive, full of mercy and good fruit, impartial and sincere. Peacemakers who sow in peace raise a harvest of righteousness.' James 3:17-18.

14th June

I recently came across a wee ditty I wrote thirty three years ago. I hadn't been married very long and... well I think the verse explains it all!

Dear Sir!

I hate to cause a stir, even less to drop a clanger.
But, I have found a smallish hair inside your famous banger!

I've been married nearly three months and to cook I've learned at last!
His favourite dish, a British pride, a comforting repast.

He's six foot tall and very large, so you can imagine the frightening crash
When I served his tea, to his dismay with hairy bangers for his mash.

So I ask you to excuse me, if I write to you in anger,
But, really Sir, would your wife serve you a hairy banger?

Jackie Doherty 1976.

15th June

CHURCH NOTICE BOARD

The visiting preachers for the following month will all be pinned up on this noticeboard in due course.

16th June

Many people may not have heard of Christina Rossetti 1830 - 1894, indeed I can never remember reading anything of hers at school, but came to know of her much later quite by chance.

Born in London to a well placed family, her father was a professor, and an Italian political asylum seeker. The family suffered financially as a result of his failing eyesight, physical and mental health. She certainly was a prominent writer of her day, writing poems, nursery rhymes, stories and letters and had a deep faith in God. She worked as a volunteer for many years at a house of charity in London.

She began writing from an early age and was first published at the age of 31.

A very famous poem of hers was set to music by Gustav Holst and today all over the world at Christmas her Carol is sung by thousands of people. More amazingly is how those haunting words affect the person reading or singing them.

Christina Rossetti could never have imagined the impact her written work would have.

The very simple words of the last verse of *'In The Bleak Mid Winter'* read:

> *What can I give Him*
> *Poor as I am*
> *If I were a shepherd*
> *I would bring a lamb*
> *If I were a wise man*
> *I would do my part*
> *Yet what I can I give Him*
> *Give, my heart.*

17th June

I was told recently about a group of women who were talking about which Bible translation they liked the best. They mentioned various translations from *'The Message'* to *'The King James'* Bible and various ones in between, when one of the younger women piped up; 'I liked my mother's translation the most, she lived it'.

18th June

'A happy mother makes a happy home.'

19th June

Have you ever noticed that if someone drives slower than you they're an idiot!

And if they drive faster they're a maniac!!

Oops! Quick read on!

20th June

'But the fruit of the Spirit is love, joy, peace, longsuffering, gentleness, goodness, faith.' Galatians 5:22.

....

21st June

Longest day of the year.

THE ONLY REASON.

The only reason women are bad drivers is because men taught them!!

Men drivers really madden me, make me really want to shout
They truly imagine they rule the roads and throw their weight about.

So I entered for a rally and put them to the test,
I thought 'I'll show these big heads who really is the best'

'Just beginners luck' they jeered and didn't drink my toast
It hurt them to give me a trophy as I'd pipped them to the post.

Even my beloved scoffed, said it wasn't really hard!
From that day on the rally club hung a sign -'WOMEN DRIVERS BARRED.'

'Oh! Well' I thought never mind I must have proved a point
By virtue of the very fact I'm not allowed inside the joint!

One day travelling down the motorway the skies began to snow
My husband motioned 'pull in dear, I'd better drive you know'

I was sure of his intention, his train of thought quite clear
He'd no faith in my driving! No confidence just fear!!

On reaching home, I just went in, put the kettle on for tea
Good heavens! I shrieked now what was that!?
He'd wrapped the car around the tree.

Jackie Doherty 1976.

(Don't write in!! It was written a long time ago!)

22nd June

23rd June

It's very hard for us to imagine how it was a few centuries ago for believers who were non- conformist in their faith. Many of the great men of faith that we know today suffered on account of their belief and many were imprisoned. So it was for the father of Isaac Watts 1674 - 1748 who was imprisoned twice for being a non-conformist!

Isaac, who was raised in Southampton, was a very bright young man and learned Greek, Hebrew, Latin and French. Such was his ability that a doctor offered to pay for young Isaac to go to Oxford or Cambridge, but because he wouldn't renounce his non-conformity he was denied access.

He was such a gifted thinker and wrote well over 500 hymns, two of his best known ones are probably 'When I Survey the Wondrous Cross' and 'Joy to the World.'

He was a pastor, a preacher, a poet, and prolific hymn writer in addition he wrote a tome on metaphysics, a major work on Astronomy, and a text book on logic that was used, ironically, at Oxford, Cambridge and Harvard for years. So diverse were his works that no other 'thinker' to date has been credited with being able to have done some of these great things as well as devising age related catechisms for children.

He was an astonishing man, he suffered for his beliefs, his hymns caused outrage in the church! They were too modern!!

He could never have known let alone imagine that his hymns would fill every type of hymn book, not only up and down the country but all over the world!

Over three hundred years later we sing out his words, written, under such great protest and harsh criticism, and give no thought to the man.

Next time we sing an Isaac Watts hymn, let's give thanks.

24th June

Midsummers Day

I don't know about you, but for my part I love to hear how individuals came to faith, I find it fascinating how people are drawn, how hearts are changed, how lives are reshaped.

As a baby I was baptised in a Presbyterian Church, from three to sixteen I attended a Methodist Church, and was confirmed at age 12. My mother had Baptist roots and my father was Jewish. As an adult I had a believers baptism in Amesbury Baptist church, and I'm married to a Catholic !! Is that eclectic list ecumenical or not!

As a result I am able to worship God in any church, indeed anywhere, which is just as well having moved around over the past thirty eight years!

I thank God for all the different denominations and it's fantastic to see Believers in every Church.

Just counting up, I've attended over 12 varieties from my early days from Church of England to Baptist, Elim Pentecostals, Church of Scotland, Free Church, and so on. Not by choice but because that is where God landed me (with a bit of help from the military!). But it was in the back of a small church in a military camp in Krefeld, Germany that I finally felt God's call upon my life and fight against it as I did I could no longer resist.

Without any shadow of a doubt the seeds of faith were sown in Sunday school, school and the life of my mother, lessons that would stay with me for life.

It is in the dark periods of my life that scripture verses come to me, examples from the Bible that I learned as a child, come rushing back to comfort, to nurture, to encourage, to give wisdom in any given situation.

The camp had once been a German Light Reconnaissance Unit during the second world war.

Looking back over my life I see so clearly (now) how God and His Holy Spirit had been prompting me many times, you may have a similar 'story.'

The 'story' I've learnt, as yet, has no end, yet for each one of us although our stories are oh so different, in many ways, they are oh, so, the same.

How great is our God!

....

25th June

'I expect to pass through life but once, if therefore, there be any kindness I can show, or any good thing I can do for my fellow being, let me do it now, for I shall not pass this way again.'

William Penn.

....

26th June

A lawyer was distraught with his dishonest client.

'I don't believe it! You've just sent a case of Moet to the judge in your hearing! That judge is as straight as an arrow, now we are sure to lose.'

'Chill, said the client, 'I sent it in the prosecutor's name.'

27th June

'These are the things you are to do; Speak the truth to each other, and render true and sound judgement in your courts,' declares the Lord.'

Zechariah 8:16.

28th June

IT WAS ONLY A LITTLE LIE

It was only a little lie,
But it had a GREAT impact,
It rippled out amazingly
Ruining integrity in fact.

It was only a small white lie
But it travelled far and wide
Causing untold heartbreak,
from which the liar couldn't hide.

It was only a tiny half truth
that misled a thousand fold.
Creating havoc where it could
while TRUTH remained untold.

As Truth was pulling on her boots
The lie had journeyed round
It was only a teeny weeny lie
But no truth was in it found.

Oh! What a web of misery
The little lie did spin
And don't we know the proper name for
Lying? Yes, it's Sin.

Jackie Doherty. 2009.

99

29th June

The new minister was trying to encourage the congregation to read their Bibles more and one Sunday announced that the following Sunday he would be speaking about LYING. He added that it would be a good thing if they could come prepared and asked them to read Romans Chapter 17.

The following Sunday just before he was to deliver his sermon he asked for a show of hands of those who had read the said passage.

Many of the congregation raised their hand.

"Right!" said the minister, "since there is no 17th chapter in Romans, I shall now begin my sermon about lying... "

30th June

Frances Ridley Havergal (1836 - 1879), poet, hymn and devotional writer, was a gifted daughter of a church of England minister, who himself was a poet and musician.

At seven she began writing verse, her mother died when she was only 11 and it's reported that she committed her life to Christ at age 14.

Although she was cultured and well educated she had a simple faith. Her health was frail and she died at the age of forty two.

Probably, her most famous hymn, which is one of my very favourites is titled:

'Take My Life and Let it Be'. For me, it is more of a prayer and one that we cannot sing too often. The words are wonderful. Written more than a hundred years ago it can speak volumes into our hearts today. Let her words be the prayer on our own lips today.

JULY

1st July

Ah! The 1st July already dear reader! I hope it's a beautiful day and you are able to make the most of it! Time passes so quickly and already we are half way through the year! Where did it go?

I'm forever texting my children to encourage them to enjoy the day –'carpe diem '– it's a phrase we know and love, and although days come and go with unfailing regularity, we can be sure that this day will never come again and that we shouldn't waste it, not a minute of it.

Is there a kindness that could be shown to another fellow human being?

Is there a need known to us where we could help?

Is there a hurting person somewhere that would benefit from our time?

Let's ask God to show us where we can help someone today.

....

2nd July

'Let us do something beautiful for God.' Mother Teresa

....

3rd July

The teenager danced about in the shop, ecstatic with her intended purchase, a little black dress. Finally she asked the salesgirl "I love it, it's perfect. But if I keep the receipt can I bring it back in case my mother likes it?"

4th July

'I have learned to be content whatever the circumstances. I know what it is to be in need, and I know what it is to have plenty. I have learned the secret of being content in any and every situation, whether well fed or hungry, whether living in plenty or in want. I can do everything through Christ who gives me strength.' Philippians 4:11-13.

5th July

OLD FAITHFUL

In these days of fashions changing and the lengths forever ranging
There's a garment every well dressed girl should own
Wear it long or wear it short, wear it as you think you ought!
Doesn't matter if it's Haute 'C' or home sewn!

It will never let you down if you're shopping in the town
Nor will it leave you feeling overdressed
With the pearls it feels just great, with a hat it turns heads straight
Leaving others most suitably impressed.

Formal moments - just the thing! Office party? - makes it swing!
Adding this or that can change its' style completely.
Whether dining, wining, dancing or just plain old romancing
"New dress?" non - committingly smile sweetly!

Worn with flatties, heels, stillettoes, worn in palaces or ghettoes
There's a code unwrit in every woman's heart.
You can keep your reds and greens, your whites and aubergines
But a woman and her 'black' must never part!

It's advice that's given early to every Sue and Shirley
No wardrobe is complete without this friend
Other clothes may rot and leave you
and as fashions change they'll grieve you
But old faithful will be there until the end.

When your hair is black and flowing or when it's grey and slowly going
The black will lend itself, in ways dramatic.
If you're too thin or too fat then just add some this or that
Altering the shape in ways now more dramatic!

You can be belt-y, scarf-y, bead-y, though never being greedy!
It's amazing just how much this dress you'll change
Whether trendy, chic or classic, into leather, suede or plastic
This number s- t- r- e- t- c- h- e- s well beyond the range.

You could wear it to the races or other interesting places
It would be that one could wear it anywhere
It's investment at its best, you could disregard the rest
There's no excuse for ever going bare!

So! If you love clothes like me then it's plain as plain can be!!
There's one thing that we should go and do right NOW
That's to discreetly 'ditch' the black or at least try and take it back
As it's jeopardising wardrobe growth and how!!

Jackie Doherty

103

6th July

....

7th July

Who can't have heard, if not sung *'Blessed Redeemer'* *'Blessed Assurance'* or *'To God be the Glory'*. These are just a few of our 'old favourite' hymns written by Fanny Crosby 1820 - 1915. She was a poet and hymn writer and wrote copiously. It's written that she produced... now! are you ready for this!... over 8,000 hymns!!

Fanny was both a pupil, first and then teacher, at the same school, The New York Institute for the Blind and dedicated herself in later life to serving the poorest and neediest people. She never let her Blindness keep her from doing anything and was very famous in her time. She had three Presidents of America as friends and died at age 94. Her first book of poems published was called *'The Blind Girl and other Poems.'*

When it comes to living a life in service to God under difficult circumstances and hardship we could all take a leaf out of her book!

....

8th July

It's the age of the e-mail, the age of the text on a mobile phone, few people ever write a letter these days, if it were possible for me to ask you, dear reader, when it was you last wrote a personal letter? Would it be this month, last month, last year?

I have always enjoyed letter writing, even as a child and was therefore thrilled some time ago to read of *'The League of the Golden Pen'* and that a group of people had made a promise to write a letter at least once a month to either encourage or uplift a friend, stranger or family member.

I don't know if the league still exists today but what a lovely thing to do.

9th July

'It is for us to pray not for tasks equal to our powers, but for powers equal to our tasks; to go forward with a great desire forever beating at the door of our hearts as we travel toward our distant goal.'

Helen Keller.

10th July

The Brigadier was hosting a cocktail party for all the people in the camp who worked in a supporting role, some of whom he had never met. He greeted each arrival with intense interest and then introduced each guest by name after shaking their hand. One chap approached him, they exchanged the usual pleasantries and the Brigadier asked him his name, to which the nervous man replied

"Made your shirts, Brigadier!!"

The host, who was hard of hearing, declared,

"May I introduce to you, Major Schurtz!"

11th July

'Therefore, as we have opportunity, let us do good to all people, especially to those who belong to the family of believers.' Galatians 6:10.

12th July

THE CHARITY SHOP

You may shop uptown in Harrods! Or indulge yourself in gay 'Paree'
But, there's one place beyond them both, a home from home, for me.
It's a place of sheer distinction, where well dressed gals should flock...
To pick selected items... a hat... a skirt... a frock.

Mixed Blessings

Perhaps an item for the boudoir, a trinket to place on show
A cook book or a thriller… a ski suit, for the snow.
There's a multitude of bargains to be found inside these stores
But grip your purse and keep it closed when you step inside their doors!

But much more than all the bargains are the ladies there each week
Who add their own vivaciousness, go yourselves and take a peek.
Now I can speak only as I find, the ladies whom I know
Who work so very diligently, to give the place its 'go'.

Each lady has her own style and adds a third dimension.
To the workload and endless pricing, about which we'll make no mention.
They share a lot of hard work, they share a lot of laughs
They raise a lot of money and I'm sure they've made some gaffes.

They may get the odd wee bargain too, with their ever present smile
And they're helping others to help others, that's a job in truth worthwhile
Their small vain little effort to help in this vast relentless world
May go quietly unnoticed until the Book of Life's unfurled.

But before we all get serious there's just one thing I'd like to say.
Have you been in the Charity Shop? Were there any bargains in today?

Jackie Doherty 1992.

13th July

14th July

Have you stayed in a hotel lately dear reader? Chances are there will have been a Bible in your bedside cupboard.

Did you ever wonder how it got there?

The Bible in the room in which you stayed, was there because of a God - incidence which occurred over one hundred years ago in a Wisconsin hotel room. One night in 1898, a travelling shoe salesman booked into a busy hotel, The Central Hotel at Boscobel, Wisconsin and was given a room, room 19, a plaque hangs there today, but the man John Nicholson, was told that he would have to share, the other man was Samuel Hill, a paint salesman.

Because of a promise to his dying mother, made when he was a young teenager, that he would read her Bible every day of his life. John told Samuel that it was his custom to read a portion of scripture each night, to which Samuel responded, that he too, was a Christian.

During the time of prayer and fellowship that followed began a bond between them, but they didn't meet again until the following year and were joined by another travelling salesman Will Knights, they decided to begin a 'Gideon' association, a fellowship for travelling salesmen away from home the name was taken from chapters 6 and 7 of Judges, a book in the Old Testament of the Bible. Eventually in 1908 the 'Gideons' were officially founded. Today they are the oldest Christian business and professional men's Association. Each year more than 56 million Bibles are distributed to hotels, prisons, hospitals and many other places worldwide. Billions and billions of Bibles in over 83 languages!

Would any of us be happy if we had to share a hotel room with a stranger? I think not!

Would we be brave enough to say to that stranger that we had a custom...

I'm not sure!

The next time something 'uncomfortable' happens, (and we know, don't we, that we won't have to wait too long before it does!) then, we'd be wise to remember who to trust in those circumstances, it may just be a God-incidence! Happy Travelling on the journey of life, fellow traveller!

15th July

The church I attended as a child was, as I recall, a very busy church, always had 'things' going on. One of my favourites was the ubiquitous round of jumble sales and of course, the white elephant stall. (I still have a large blue and white meat platter bought for three pence when I was a little girl.)

Today we have charity shops and car boot sales, auctions and the like, our television screens show a multiplicity of programmes ranging from The Antiques Roadshow to Flog it!

I enjoy auctions, car boots and charity shops and during our time in the military I have voluntarily managed and helped in many 'Thrift Shops' over the years. It's jolly hard work!

I went to my first car boot sale about thirty years ago now and no matter where we have lived, abroad or at home, there have been an abundance of these type of events call them what you will...flea markets, trodelmarkets etc.

I have so many lovely stories concerning my times at these events and would like to tell you about just one of them.

It was a lovely day, an early start, and I noticed out the corner of my beady eye, a man with a most wonderful collection of ladies' clothes of excellent quality. Quickly, there gathered a scramble at his pitch, of women trying to pick up a bargain, he certainly had many bargains for the taking that day as I learnt each jumper was only 50p. Although his 'stock' was wonderful it was just not to my personal taste or size. The man had a thunderous air about him and was not a happy man at all and I wondered what had brought him there that day with just ladies' clothes. I shall never know the answer to that but had thought he was taking some delight in shifting his stock so quickly, his manner intimated that for some reason (perhaps revenge?) he was glad to 'get rid of it.'

I did notice a beautiful trench coat that I liked very much and examined it, great quality, hardly worn at all, I'd thought, and timidly asked how much, fearful of having my head bitten off, surely this wasn't 50p like everything else on the pitch, he caught my frightened gaze and knew he had a sale and answered that it was a pound.

All around me was mayhem, women pushing and shoving, laden with armfuls of good quality gear at 50p a piece.

I was happy to give a pound for my great bargain and tried to give him a smile. Somehow I imagined I felt his unknown pain, the smile was never returned.

At home I tried the coat on it was even better than I'd remembered, however it was just too big, but I knew instantly who would love it, my mother-in-law Dolly. As I put my hand in the pocket I felt a piece of paper and pulled my hand out with a £5 pound note!

That day in Church, the collection got an extra fiver (it was just too far to take the fiver back to the man, though that was what I dearly wanted to do) the unhappy man was prayed for and Dolly got a fab new coat! Bargains all round.

16th July

'He is no fool who gives what he cannot keep, to gain what he cannot lose.'

17th July

Firemen and an ambulance crew were frantically working to remove the driver from the front seat after his car had been struck by an overtaking lorry. The emergency workers could hear him sobbing 'my Mercedes, oh, my Mercedes!'

Trying to placate the distressed man in order to get him out of the vehicle before it burst into flames, somewhat stressed an experienced fireman said, 'Sir, don't worry about your car! We need to get you out, I'm sorry to tell you that your right arm has been severed below the elbow and we need to get you out of this vehicle NOW.'

The driver went quiet… and then he began 'My Rolex, my poor Rolex!'

18th July

'Good will come to him who is generous and lends freely, who conducts his affairs with justice.' Psalm 112:5.

19th July

THE CAR BOOT SALE

It's early morn the sun's abed, there's money in my pocket
I grab an apple for the road and am dressed like Davy Crockett,
All layered up with boots and hat, a torch to lead the way
An empty bag to hold the goods, that I'll be taking home today.

Parking in a farmer's field, the smell of dew filled earth
The squish of mud beneath my feet, I know my footwear's worth.
A frosty chill is in the air, the punters all are cheery
The forecast's not a glorious one, in fact it's rather dreary.

But that won't stop the buyers, nor the sellers, that's a fact!
As you hear again for the hundredth time 'that's new' 'never used' 'it's intact!'
You'll also hear a lot of...'what's the best you'll do on that'
Or 'I can't go lower than... ' some extortionate price... for tat!

Then in other quiet corners, you'll find a wondrous thing
An item you've been searching for, which makes your heart just sing.
You discover a book of beauty on sale for just 10p
You wouldn't dream of haggling, on any price you would agree.

A cup of tasteless coffee next in the half light of the day
(Which cost more than the tasteful book you bought) you throw most of it away
You look over all your purchases check the cash flow and the hour
Before whipping round one last time, to beat an early morning shower.

Happy with the hunting, joyous from the find
satisfied with the gathering, it's time to leave the field behind.

Jackie Doherty

20th July

WHY DID THE FISH CROSS THE ROAD?

TO GET TO THE OTHER TIDE!!

21st July

Fyodor Dostoyevsky 1821 - 1881 was a Russian journalist, writer, essayist and philosopher who is widely recognised as one of the greatest writers of all time. It is written that Tolstoy wept when he heard of his death and that over 4,000 people attended his funeral.

An epileptic, he suffered from seizures and poor health and although he was a popular literary writer of much acclaim at the young age of 24, he didn't have an easy life at all, even to the end.

He knew personally of hardship and perhaps this is what gave him the ability to reach out and touch his readers' hearts.

Probably his best known novel was *'Crime and Punishment'* (1866).

He was sentenced to death in 1849 for his part in supposed revolutionary activities but at the last minute his sentence was reprieved by the Czar, Nicholas I and instead he was sentenced to ten years hard labour at a penal colony in Siberia, but served only four of them before his release.

It's written that he commenced his journey there on Christmas Eve and that at some point of his journey he was handed a copy of the New Testament by two women who told him to search its pages carefully. He discovered between the pages twenty five roubles, but much more than the money he found, were 'riches' beyond compare. The words he read therein were to sustain him throughout his arduous times in Siberia and also upon his return which was far from easy.

Following his time in Siberia almost every piece of his literature refers to God and especially the parable of the Prodigal Son, which he weaves almost into every piece of his later work.

I cannot contemplate how hard his life was and how he must have suffered and often feel that it is glamorised somehow, but despite all the injustice and suffering he was able to see God's hand in it and then was able to use his gift of writing, to present it to the world through his works.

Perhaps... and we don't know this, but just perhaps this all came about as a result of him being given the New Testament by two women, two strangers...

Who knows... ?

22nd July

Many years ago, my husband's aunt gave us a little brown vase she had made at her pottery class in Cornwall, it was quite pretty and in the style of slipware, not really to my taste.

One day, about 15 years later, before another move, I decided to 'do' a car boot sale and have a clear out. A man rushed over and bought the said vase, clearly thinking it was something important. Some years later, in a different part of the country, I was at an auction and was bidding blind (buying without having checked the item first!) for a box of pottery that had a huge blue teapot on the top, which had taken my fancy!

The hammer went down, mine, at a fair price and eventually I got the box home. Unpacking it, I discovered a few good finds but none so surprising as finding my old brown vase!

Needless to say I will never part with it again!

23rd July

'The only thing we have to fear... is fear itself.'

Roosevelt.

24th July

The plumber had just finished the emergency work and handed the lady a bill for £350, at which she gasped, "£350 for less than an hours work! Why that is ridiculous, my husband is a banker and he doesn't earn that much!"

The plumber remained straight faced as he replied "No, neither did I when I was a banker!"

25th July

'"I know the plans I have for you," declares the Lord, "plans to prosper you and not to harm you, plans to give you hope and a future."'

Jeremiah 29:11

26th July

THE CAR BOOT SALE AS A SELLER

The alarm shrills out, it's early morn. I rise to greet the day
The car's all packed, no room to spare. At four I'm on my way.
The farmer's fields awash with cars, all queuing for a spot
I just relax and wait my turn, thinking of things I may have forgot!
Yes! I've brought the table, loose change, paper, labels and the stuff!
Bags, tissues, apples, mobile phone, a pen, sarnies, loo roll
(in case there's not enough!)
The place is filling up now! I'm checked into my place
The buyers all crowd round me invading body space!
It's almost six, the dealers pounce, with torches on head and hand
Trying to get something for nothing and finding treasures rare unplanned.
The dawn arrives, the hordes thin out, It's time to catch a break
A yawn, a sneeze in the chill morn air, and check the growing cash flow intake.
Eleven am my stocks decreased, the end is now in sight
Time to have a well earned rest a drink and a bacon bite.
Almost everything I brought has sold on to owners many,
The car will go home empty and I've earned a pretty penny!
It was waste not, want not, there today, recycling all the way.
Home now, shattered… worn out… tired, an exhausting de-cluttering day.

Jackie Doherty.

27th July

28th July

A most wonderful, true and well documented story that I never tire of hearing is one told by Bishop Desmond Tutu, Nobel Peace Prize 1984, so much so, that every single time I hear the bishop's name, I remember the story.

When he was a young boy living in Africa, where his father was a teacher and his mother worked in a School for the blind, he witnessed some act of human kindness that would stay in his memory forever.

One day, he was standing in the street with his mother when a white man in priest's clothing walked past. As he passed, he took his hat off to 'doff' it, so the expression goes, to young Tutu's mother. The child could not believe his eyes! A white man who greeted a black working class woman!!

This event had an astounding effect upon the young boy.

The white man to whom he refers is the late Archbishop Trevor Huddleston.

Quite apart from all the great and inspiring achievements of these two great men over the years, it is one small gesture of kindness and respect to a fellow human being, the very small gesture of raising a hat, that underpins their greater gestures.

My mother always told us as children, that civility costs nothing. I would add that it can, as this true story shows, mean everything.

29th July

I read somewhere once that Sir Humphry Davy, 1778 - 1829 English Chemist, Scientist, the man who is probably best known for having invented the safety lamp, used by miners, once said:

'Life is not made up of great sacrifices or duties, but of little things, in which smiles and kindnesses and small obligations given habitually are what win and preserve the hearts and secure comfort.'

30th July

'Nothing costs as much as caring... except not caring.'

31st July

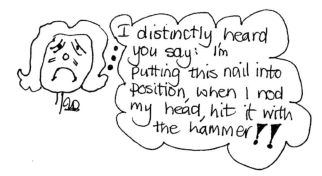

Mixed
Blessings

AUGUST

1st August

'Who shall separate us from the love of Christ? Shall trouble or hardship or persecution or famine or nakedness or danger or sword? No, in all these things we are more than conquerors through Him who loved us. For I am convinced that neither death nor life, neither angels nor demons, neither the present nor the future, nor any powers, neither height nor depth, nor anything else in all creation, will be able to separate us from the love of God that is in Christ Jesus our Lord.'

Romans 8:35, 37-39.

2nd August

The following poem was written when I was a student nurse in the seventies, although prompted by my compassion for a dear patient, wondering what he may have been feeling, I believe now it was a 'prompting' of the Holy Spirit, as I look back, I believe I was seeking God.

WHY

> *I went to bed with peace of mind,*
> *the nurses are so very kind*
> *But I wish they'd say when I can go,*
> *for I am a busy man you know!*
> *These are the thoughts I once did think,*
> *when sipping slowly my last drink*
> *The lights went out and so to sleep...*
> *I prayed the Lord my soul to keep...*

… It must be six, the lights are on.
Oh! How I'd enjoy to linger on

To lay in bed is such a treat,
an hour longer off my feet.

But alas! The nurse must do her rounds
and soon I'll hear familiar sounds

The chink of the cups, the turn of the key
into the trolley for drugs for me

I'd better get up… they've a lot to do,
besides I'd enjoy a cup of their brew!

What a blessing it is to suffer no pain!
And I try to sit up but find it a strain.

Oh! My leg feels so stiff.
can't lift my arm,

I feel my heart race,
yet I can't raise an alarm.

I open my mouth to utter my fears.
I shout and I shout yet nobody hears!

The nurse races past and I try to call out,
she bellows "GOOD MORNING!" and dashes about.

I gulp and suspect that I've laid wrong in bed,
but hope is soon lost as my right side seems dead.

I lift up my left arm and feel for my right,
it's there I can feel it. Yes! It will soon be alright.

I've got to be dreaming - a quick rush of fear, oh!
Why can't that nurse keep still and come here?

One side has no feeling - I can't raise my head,
no! it's just pins and needles, I've laid wrong in bed!

"MORNING TO YOU! AND HOW DO YOU FEEL?"
She briskly remarks and turns on her heel,

"OPEN WIDE NOW AND LET'S POP THIS IN,
I'M RUNNING BEHIND" she says with a grin.

"COM'ON NOW DEAR MAN 'N DO AS I SAY
Y' KNOW WE'RE BUSY, IT'S THE BIG ROUND TODAY"

She asks how I've slept and why I don't speak
then stares quite in awe at the tear on each cheek

Two paces back and her hand on the bell,
by the look on her face I can tell all's not well.

The Staff Nurse arrives, they've had a bad night
and now they are faced with a pitiful sight.

"How d'you feel Mr X?" They both exclaim,
then wait a few moments and repeat it again

They lower their voices and turn to one side,
then turn back and smile...their horror to hide.

One rushes off and the other remains,
Oh, Lord, what I'd give to feel one of those pains!!

There never has been an unluckier bloke.
Oh! Lord WHY did I, have this stroke?

Night sister arrives "Now what's going on?"
She fumbles a bit and then she is gone.

Why has it happened? I'm not even old!
Won't somebody please give me their hand to hold?

They talk all around me as though I were dead,
discussing what happened inside of my head

They prod me all over and expose me to all, I
glance at my torso, my pose is a sprawl!

The day passed so quickly, I slept with the drugs,
my wife came to see me, no kisses no hugs.

It was plain from her face that I'd ruined our life,
what have I now... no job and no wife.

Lots of things happened in between induced sleep
and various bodies saw a shattered man weep

My tears flowed so freely, when I lay there awake
and I prayed to the Lord. My soul please... to take.

But it wasn't the will of my creator I fear,
yet what earthly use am I? Lying thus here?

They feed me and clothe me, brush teeth and hair,
shave me and bathe me... it's called nursing care.

And so I have worked all my life without ease,
ending unable to utter yes, no or please.

These lips that have kissed and these hands that have held
can no longer work and are action repelled.

... and day in and day out... as the years pass me by,
I'm bitter, resentful, unable to cry.

Why didn't I bleed enough to then die?
The question I ask is only... Lord... WHY?

Jackie Doherty October 1976

119

3rd August

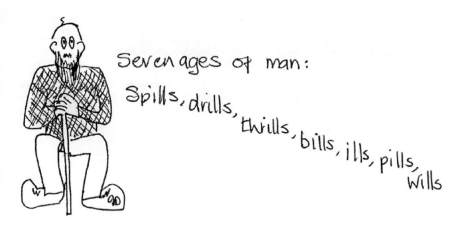

Seven ages of man:
Spills, drills, thrills, bills, ills, pills, wills

....

4th August

For most of my growing up life my mother would often tell me about a book she loved very much and only wished that I would be able to read it too. She had often read it to her younger sister and then been scolded by their mother for making her sister cry. Sadly, like so many other people their home was bombed (three times in total during the war years!) and the 'book' was lost to a memory! At family gatherings and such the 'book' would be mentioned over and over with much fondness!

Some years later, as a grown woman, I was in an auction in the Salisbury area and happened to glance over a crate of books in an old fashioned packing carton, a tea chest type, when to my utter delight and disbelief I saw the very book that I'd been searching for all my life, there on the top! I was in a panic because I knew that I just had to buy it, but was dreading what the whole 'lot' would cost. I was even more amazed to have purchased the entire crate of books for an amazing £2!!

There were many collectable books in that crate even a first edition Henty, but none was more precious to me than *'Her Benny'*, I couldn't wait to tell my mother!

As soon as I was able I sat and read the book, it is a children's book but has a message for every seeking heart.

It was published in 1879 and is set in Liverpool and beyond and was written by Silas K Hocking a Methodist minister born in Cornwall (1850 - 1935) who worked in the north west of England for a time.

He was the first ever author to sell a million of his books in his own lifetime! (his brother was also a famous author). Silas wrote over 50 books in total and *'Her Benny'* was his second book. He also became a politician in the Liberal Party.

Over the years I have acquired a few of his books and have been moved by each of them, but hold *'Her Benny'* in my heart. Each of my children have read it also and each of us have cried in so doing, the book is well tear stained! My particular copy had once been a Sunday school gift for someone in 1903 from the Congregational Church in Sherborne, Dorset for good attendance.

I often wonder how many people have read and been moved deeply by this book. A simple story of Victorian Liverpool based on real characters, of whom Silas Hocking says in his preface 'I knew these people well.'

5th August

I love the story, and hope you will too, about the lady who was always grumbling.

When she died an angel gave her a tour and showed her so many wonderful things, beautiful places, waterfalls, mountains, forests, flowers, laughing children, singing birds, animals galore, haunting music, happy music, every genre of music, rushing waves, sunsets and sunrises, one glorious sight after the other was before her eyes.

'Oh! How marvellous heaven is!' she said to the angel.

'Heaven? No this is the world where you lived but never saw!' said the puzzled angel.

Of course it is only a story, but one we all need to hear, every now and again.

6th August

A philosophy of life.

Life is an opportunity, benefit from it.
Life is a beauty, admire it.
Life is bliss, taste it.
Life is a dream, realise it.
Life is a challenge, meet it.
Life is a duty, complete it.
Life is a game, play it.
Life is costly, care for it.
Life is wealth, keep it.
Life is love, enjoy it.
Life is mystery, know it.
Life is a promise, fulfil it.
Life is sorrow, overcome it.
Life is a song, sing it.
Life is a struggle, accept it.
Life is a tragedy, confront it.
Life is an adventure, dare it.
Life is too precious, do not destroy it.
Life is life, fight for it!

Mother Teresa of Calcutta.

7th August

It's so important to make the most of 'life', take my neighbour, for example, she wanted to stay fit and started walking 2 miles every day at the age of fifty.

She must be sixty now and we haven't a clue where she is!!

8th August

Jesus said, 'I tell you the truth, he who believes has everlasting life.'
John 6:47.

9th August

INSPIRING FOLK

Throughout the pages of this book,
I've mentioned fine inspiring folk
Who've brought much comfort, joy and love,
to those, whose hearts are broke.

With words that touch our inner heart,
that cause us to seek out God's face
Mostly written through their own pain,
can testify to His saving Grace.

We may not endure their painful lives,
perhaps not share all their sorrows
But their words, stories, poems, books,
light our paths for unknown tomorrows.

'Tis said 'the pen is mightier',
for there's power in the written word
And in the Bible even more so,
as it acts like a two-edged sword.

The verses we learnt as children,
come back, time'n time again.
To encourage, remind and reprove us,
as we need it now and then.

We may never be a 'great one',
but we too must play our part
And learn to serve where we're planted,
with a willing servant's heart.

For each of us has a purpose,
in God's wider mighty plan
He loves each of us like no other,
whether woman, child or man.

We are special, children of God,
privileged to be called His sons and heirs
So, no matter dear reader, what troubles you,
remember, in heaven there's no more tears.

Jackie Doherty.

123

10th August

WHY DID THE COW CROSS THE ROAD?

TO GET TO THE UDDER SIDE!

11th August

How could I ever do justice, in a few short lines, to the Wesley family for their devotion to God in their lifetimes?

Indeed whenever I think of the Wesley brothers I cannot help but think of their dear mother who had 19 children!

John Wesley, the fifteenth child, (1703 - 1791), was an Anglican who founded the Methodist movement but stayed within the Church of England. His was a fascinating childhood. Later he was troubled with profound self doubt. Both he and his brother were saved from a burning house in their childhood.

Charles Wesley (1707 - 1788), was a gifted preacher, poet, hymn writer became a leader in the Methodist church. Charles wrote more than five thousand hymns!

Both brothers worked tirelessly, often travelling long distances on horseback, to preach. They were popular preachers of their time and often suffered critical words because of their teaching. They both had a tremendous education and could have been anything they wanted to be, but each independent of the other chose to serve God at a cost, oftentimes to themselves.

How can I single out a most famous hymn when there are so many to choose from? 'Love Divine all Loves Excelling' is just one hymn or poem which portrays God's love. Born over three centuries ago Charles Wesley's influence is all around us today.

12th August

Recently I was due an update on my *'Moving and Handling'* certificate as required by all nursing staff on a regular basis.

One of the basic rules in lifting is to bend one's knees and not one's back!

During a quiet moment some time later I was thinking about that process and likened it to life, in that it often is not so much what we are 'carrying' but how we are 'carrying it'.

How very true for life's worries... how we 'carry' them can bring us more harm.

13th August

'Make all you can. Save all you can. Give all you can.'

John Wesley.

14th August

A little girl was running very fast to school in order that she wouldn't be late again.

Every so often she would pray 'Please God don't let me be late... '

Suddenly she was running so fast that she lost her footing and fell over, as she was dusting herself off she prayed :

'Please God don't let me be late... but please don't push.'

15th August

'Cast your cares on the Lord and He will sustain you; He will never let the righteous fall.'

Psalm 55:22.

125

16th August

ANTS.

Have you ever watched an ant? Rushing briskly on his way -
Have you wondered that he wonders what he'll do with each new day?

Have you ever killed an ant and stopped his life in pain
With one tread of your foot he will never crawl again.

Did the little chap have family? Even children in the nest!
Yet you killed him without feeling for you regard him as a pest.

This tiny little creature
Did not harm you nor provoke
He merely went about his business
And he hardly ever spoke...
No... no... not in words as you and I can
Nor in language that we'd know
But these ants can communicate
In more ways than we could show.

They are creatures of the earth, mites as small as small can be
Can you tell me what the threat is? What harm they cause to you and me?

Are they happy in their armies? Do they get a decent pay?
And the ants that live on foreign soil, do they speak in a different way?

Do they battle in their colonies? Have they Generals in command?
Do they merge their small battalions to share a common land?

Do they have a set commander? Do they live in moral ways?
Or do they kill each other off, living as we do these days?

What purpose has their being? What plans for them are made?
As man we just ignore them until our homes they do invade!

They work so hard - such quickness! Do they ever rest or sleep?
If I could shrink a lot of times in their nests I'd like to peep.

They have workers, royalty and feeder ants, of these facts I'm pretty sure
Although my knowledge begins and ends... when they crawl around my door!!!

And WHY... do they persist... in trying to get in?
You'd think in their own habitats they'd be content therein

By writing this odd verse, I've put my guilt to rest...
For I caught a squadron of ants today and quickly sprayed their nest!!!!

Jackie Doherty 1983.

17th August

WHAT DO YOU CALL AN ANT THAT LIVES WITH YOUR GREAT UNCLE?

A GREAT A(U)NT!

WHAT DO YOU CALL AN ANT THAT MISSES SCHOOL?

A TRUANT!

18th August

Horatio Bonar (1808 - 1889) was yet another prolific poet, writer, hymn writer, preacher, he was born from a line of ministers in Edinburgh, Scotland.

One of his well known hymns is *'I Heard the Voice of Jesus Say'*, which is still popular today.

It's written of Bonar that he was an earnest student of prophecy.

Among his many written works is a piece called *'God's Way of Peace.'*

127

19th August

Several years ago now, terribly troubled and anxious, I had been praying for many things. It was a beautiful day, I was on a day off from work, we were living in Dorset at the time and I felt drawn to drive into Weymouth for some inexplicable reason.

On arrival, I didn't park where I normally would and approached that beautiful town from a different, unknown direction. I parked easily, the drive there had done little to stem the fast flowing tears and because of them I decided not to go into the centre of the town just then and headed off across a bridge, where to, I didn't know or much care.

I have been to Weymouth many, many times in my life and had never ventured over this walkway before mainly because it seems to lead nowhere and away from the town itself.

As I crossed the bridge, I spotted a tiny Christian Bookshop over on the other side of the road and crossed over, on entering the shop the first book that I picked up was a book by Horatio Bonar, it was a very thin book, I had thought it was called 'Why Christians Suffer' but it was probably called 'When God's Children Suffer.'

Standing alone in that book shop, reading what had been written a century before, for Christians and probably non Christians alike, brought peace to my aching heart. It didn't solve one of the many concerns, not one, but it changed my attitude toward them. Just words in an old book, yet as powerful as though they had been spoken to me. The Author could never have known just how poignant his words could be, a century or so after he wrote them.

....

20th August

Three things which cannot be recalled:

A spoken word
A sped arrow
Missed opportunity.

Persian proverb

21st August

22nd August

'Trust in the Lord with all your heart and lean not on your own understanding; in all your ways acknowledge Him, and He will make your paths straight.'

Proverbs 3:5, 6.

23rd August

This is a poem I found recently dating back to the late seventies, another seeking poem...

LOVE

There are many thoughts on loving, but what is it all about?
Surely it's just an emotion... and yet I still have a doubt.
Surely, it's more than a feeling, for someone, for whom you much care
I feel it's profound dedication, an act of just being there.

It's so easy to love when life's simple, so simple to live when in love,
But when tragedy strikes to upset this, life's shattered and the going gets tough.
It's then that love is tested and stretched to the far sublime
But may I say with experience, that this is the test of all time.

Forgive me if I start to digress, for the subjects too great to dismiss
That love is merely an emotion that can start with a romantic kiss
For there are various methods of loving, of which we've sampled a taste
Motherly, fatherly, to name just a few, yet, still, there's a terrible waste.

When did we last smile at a stranger? Or offer a helping hand
And why is it normal to 'stand back', this I simply can't understand.
We can all learn a lesson from children, whose love is pure and unstained
They love so freely and simply, even when there is nought to be gained.

Then tell me what happens to change this? As they age and reservations then grow
Do they learn from the adults around them, not to let their true feelings show.
There are so many ways of loving, but the old adage I think says it all
That, actions speak louder than words and sometimes the order's quite tall!

To care when something's unpleasant, to be there when the going gets tough
To love and give strength to a person, to me... is the real kind of love
For better for worse is a saying, so apt when uniting the pairs
For it's simple to stay when it's 'better', but better simply to stay when it's 'worse'

We should all be a little more loving and learn to trust just a little bit more
We should all have a little more feeling... after all... that's what it's there for...

Jackie Doherty.

24th August

We have two ears and one mouth, to be used in that order !

25th August

I also came across this old favourite prayer recently, I don't know when it was written but the words are timeless:

CHRIST

Has no body now on earth but yours,
No hands but yours
No feet but yours

Yours are the eyes through
Which, must look out Christ's compassion on the world.

Yours are the feet with which
He is to go about doing good.

Yours are the hands with which
He is to bless men now.

Prayer of St. Teresa.

26th August

A neighbours' daughter had been very late getting home and as soon as she turned the corner and was in sight my neighbour began to yell at her daughter, 'where have you been? I was so worried' and so on.

The child explained that she'd been playing with her friend and her dog, when the dog ran away and couldn't be found.

The mother relieved began to feel sorry for the telling off and said gently 'Oh! And you stayed to help her find her dog?'

The child replied truthfully 'No, we couldn't find it, so I just stayed and cried with her until the dog returned!'

What a friend!

131

27th August

'Correction does much but encouragement does more.' Goethe.

28th August

The Girl Guides were all settling in at camp and inspection was due, the guide leader spotted a hot water bottle, neatly hidden in the sleeping bag and asked the owner why it was there since it was definitely not on the list.

Absolutely embarrassed the red faced Guide just looked at her leader and said in despair 'That's mothers for you!'

29th August

'A friend loves at all times.'

Proverbs 17:17.

30th August

NO USE CRYING

People think inanimate objects cannot feel but they are wrong
For I'm a glass milk bottle and feel I really do belong
I've been up and down this street, in and out of many doors
Standing up in many fridges and been spilt on many floors

I've been pecked at by some birds, attacked by the cat at number one
Frozen solid by the icy weather and baked warm by the sun
I dislike going to number eight, they don't wash me very clean
They never use hot water, so all milk stains can be seen.

I'm not quite sure how old I am, but have had many Christmas morns
I've been welcomed many mornings, by some smiles and many yawns.
I like to be out at night time, in case I get forgotten
For missing a day at the dairy can sometimes be quite rotten.

Although I am fair tempered, I just cannot stand the kids
Who pick me up and take a swig and then replace the lids!!
But all in all I'm happy and pleased to be on hand
For hungry, thirsty people and the odd spill that's unplanned.

So next time dear readers when you wash and 'put me out'
Please don't leave me dirty as I like to glow when out.

Jackie Doherty 1980
(when milk came in bottles!)

31st August

The milkman was a bit surprised by the note which read 'Please leave 15 gallons of milk today, thank you.'

So, he knocked on the door and asked the lady of the house did she mean 15 'pints' of milk.

The lady explained that she was going to take a bath in the milk and so the note was correct.

Unfazed by the request, the milkman asked 'Pasteurised?'

'No,' said the woman, 'just up to my neck!'

133

M
i
x
Blessings
d

SEPTEMBER

1st September

'Thirty days hath September
April, June and November
All the rest have thirty one
Excepting February alone,
Which, has twenty eight days clear
And, twenty nine, in each Leap Year.'

Who never learnt this rhyme as a child?

I tell you, it has helped me out over the years, especially now that I'm getting older! It's what is termed a mnemonic verse, in simple terms a verse to help someone remember, something. It's an Old English poem dating back to the 16th Century!

The original, which is said to be recorded in the British Library is written in Olde English and reads differently, there are many variations of this verse, but this is the one that I can remember from my schooldays.

It's amazing that it has lasted so long! I can't help wonder if the writer ever thought, in his wildest dreams, that it would still be recited in the 21st Century?

2nd September

'Septem' is Latin for seven and September was always the seventh month of the year, in the Roman Calendar until 153 BC, when it changed and it's now the ninth month of the year.

I love the month of September for many reasons, the change in the seasons, the nights slowly drawing in, the leaves changing colour on the trees and in particular the start of new beginnings, even in the latter part of the year, in the northern hemisphere it is widely accepted as the beginning of the academic year.

Can you remember when you were at school, preparing to start afresh each September? New shoes, uniform, pencil case and other items, especially a new school bag!

For the past twelve years I have been employed, among other things, as a Sanatorium sister or a Sickbay nurse and I just love September from this point of view, to see new pupils/students arrive and to meet up with those who have grown and returned for another year, even to meet with teachers, refreshed after a well earned and much needed break.

Yes, September in school life, is an exciting time indeed, even though it is usually a very busy period for all involved, especially the young people who have to adjust to new timetables, new teachers, new peer groups, new lessons.

This September, let's spare a thought for all those who have new beginnings who are known to us. Let's support them in prayer or with a kind and caring word.

None of us naturally like 'change' and it can be very hard to articulate the worries and anxieties that change can bring to a person's heart, but when change is viewed as a new beginning it can bring encouragement and hope for better things to come.

....

3rd September

'The grass withers, the flower fades, but the word of our God stands forever.' Isaiah 40:8

4th September

It was the first day of a new term. The teacher was getting to know his new class of young pupils but couldn't quite remember the name of the boy stood right in front of him:

"And tell me, what is your name?" asked the teacher.

The boy responded "It's Matthew."

The teacher, wanting to begin on the right foot, reminded him that he should say "sir."

The boy smiled and swelled with pride: "Oh! Ok, My name is Sir Matthew."

5th September

God knows our name and more! The Bible tells us that He knows how many hairs are on our head!

'"Before I formed you in the womb I knew you, before you were born I set you apart," says the Lord.' Jeremiah 1:5

6th September

HE KNOWS MY NAME

He knows my name…
There is no need for formal introduction
He longs to hear me call His name
And read His word, His Book of good instruction.

He knows me better than I even know myself
And often like a child I try to stray
He gently takes me by the heart and mind
And whispers in still times, 'Child, come this way.'

I am no king, nor queen of high position
I'm just a sinner saved, that is my worth
But WOW! Christ died for me and my salvation
My Father loved me e'en before my birth.

137

He knows how many hairs are on my head
He knows the inner chambers of my heart
And longs for me to seek Him every moment
As He gently tries His wisdom to impart.

The angels all rejoiced at my return
The thought ...oh! I can scarcely take it in!
He also knows your name, dear reader!
Won't you open up your heart and let Him in.

Jackie Doherty

7th September

WHY DID THE FISH CROSS THE ROAD THIS TIME?

TO GET TO SCHOOL!

8th September

Of course I must confess there is another reason why I love September! It is my birthday Month!

Today is my Birthday and even though I share my birthday with my husband, I doubt very much that he will be singing *'Happy Birthday'* to me! I know for sure that my mother would sing it to me, if she were alive and fully expect my mother-in-law to ring me at the crack of dawn to give her rendition of that lovely old refrain that is sung all over the world. Indeed I always sing 'it' to my three grown children, whether they want me to or not!

It is a well recognised song indeed and has been translated into many languages. The origins of it's being, are attributed to two sisters from Kentucky, America. It was written for the Kindergarten where they worked and began life as; 'Good Morning to You' and was changed when the sisters, Mildred and Patty began singing it at family gatherings and it became the ubiquitous *'Happy Birthday to You'*.

Be very careful though not to sing it in public as it has a copyright on it! So much so that it is hardly ever used in it's entirety in films or television etc, as copyright can cost up to $10,000 reportedly!

Written as a ditty for a classroom setting, the sisters, who went on to achieve great things in their later life, could never have guessed that their few words could have achieved such notoriety or usage over a hundred years after they were written!

Mildred began her life as a kindergarten and Sunday school teacher and then became a composer, organist and pianist among other things, whilst her sister became a doctor, working for many years on the faculty at a University Teachers College in Columbia. She became a great educator.

It is reported that the current copyright under law will exist until 2030 at the earliest!

9th September

I hate to admit it, especially as I am a nurse, but my tea making skills are not the best, this is probably due to many reasons, the main one being that I am not naturally a tea drinker, I prefer coffee.

About twelve years ago I was out doing the weekly shop and had both parents staying for a few weeks at the time. We all headed off for the shops, my father, a keen tea drinker who could never pass a watering hole, insisted we began with a cuppa. This rankled me slightly, three children, a hectic day ahead, chores to be done etc, but we stopped for tea.

My parents found a seat and I went for the refreshments, distracted, I took a coffee for me and duly made two teas. It wasn't rocket science. My father asked me what it was that he was drinking, I replied it was tea, as he'd asked. 'Oh' he said puzzled 'it tastes like coffee and tea.' Confused, I tasted it and he was right! I returned to the counter and found that I'd picked up cups with coffee already in them and added tea to them! We laughed so much about that mistake that day and for years later too!

I now pay great attention to visitors when they request a cup of tea at my home, because I know that I don't make nice tea naturally, without remembering the basics of warming the pot, etc, and when I'm making the tea, I am reminded always that it's an analogy of how we should live our lives.

Often we are distracted and can easily forget the things we once learned. Tea making is a very trivial thing, but in making the best of our lives, we too become distracted by worldly ways and forget there is a 'right' way to do things, the instructions for so doing can be found in the Bible!

When we follow the manufacturers' advice in making tea, we can be sure the advice is good, likewise, when we follow our maker's instructions we're able to live a better life.

Nowadays, I only wish that I had my parents shopping with me!! I'd stop at EVERY watering hole.

....

10th September

'A cynic is a man who knows the price of everything and the value of nothing.'

Oscar Wilde.

....

11th September

....

12th September

'All Scripture is God-breathed and is useful for teaching, rebuking, correcting and training in righteousness, so that the man of God may be thoroughly equipped for every good work.' 2 Timothy 3:16.

13th September

THE BIBLE

When did you last open your Bible?
When will you then open it next?
When will you refer to the manual?
When will you read God's Holy text?

Jackie Doherty.

14th September

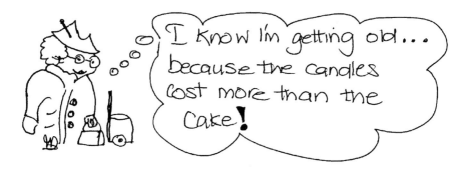

15th September

Who hasn't heard of that awesome writer C.S.Lewis?

Clive Staples Lewis (1898 - 1963) was born in Belfast. His nickname was Jack to family and friends and came about as a result of his dog, called Jacksie, whom he loved, but had died, when Lewis was a young child.

Lewis declared himself an Atheist as a teenager. He studied and later taught at Oxford where he gained an amazing triple first! He was a copious writer, academic and essayist. He did serve on the front line as an officer, during the First World War and later returned to his studies.

At Oxford he was part of the *'Inklings'* set, of which, JRR Tolkein was a member too. Whilst there, Lewis also knew Sir John Betjeman and many other now famous people.

It was there that he came again to faith and he has written that Tolkein had some influence in this area of his life.

The *'Chronicles of Narnia'* are read and seen worldwide by Christians and non Christians alike. Lewis wrote many books, poems, essays and I thoroughly recommend 'The Screwtape Letters' if you haven't already read it!

As an Atheist, Lewis could have had no idea how God would use his gift of writing for His benefit, throughout the world!

16th September

As a junk collector, I buy the odd piece because I like it. I don't mind that it doesn't bear a master craftsman's mark, unlike many serious collectors who prefer a piece that bears a maker's mark, which is a sign of a quality piece, it establishes for the collector, a reputation of good workmanship, a name to be respected and trusted. Something of worth.

C.S. Lewis wrote a piece of work called *'The Weight of Glory'* about the worth of any of us.

'There are no ordinary people.'

These few short words of his work are very powerful, when we recognise people, as made in God's image, we begin to see in them something of worth!

Lewis was right, there are NO ordinary people, each and every person is a unique piece made by the Master Craftsman's hand personally.

17th September

'A man can no more diminish God's glory by refusing to worship Him than a lunatic can put out the Sun by scribbling the word 'darkness' on the walls of his cell.'

C.S. Lewis.

18th September

The young antique dealer was so proud of his achievements, he'd moved across town and now had just moved into a swish looking shop, filled with rare finds. He noticed a potential customer arrive and picked up the telephone and started speaking into it, tutting now and then and generally giving the impression that he was a big shot in the world of antiques. After a few minutes he replaced the receiver and turned to face the man in his shop and asked if he may help him.

To which the surprised man said 'Yes, I've come to connect your telephone, Sir!'

19th September

'The fool says in his heart, "There is no God."' Psalm 53:1a.

20th September

THE LOVE

> *I own no precious jewels rare,*
> *I own no diamonds I could wear*
> *I own no riches I could share*
> *Except, the love of God.*
>
> *His love out prices diamond rings*
> *His love alone, contentment brings*
> *His love casts out the fearful things*
> *This love, the love of God.*
>
> *And I must give His love away*
> *In all I do, in all I say*
> *To know Him there's no other way*
> *To show the love, the love of God.*

Jackie Doherty

143

21st September

If we want to remove a mountain – we must start by carrying away small rocks.

....

22nd September

Every time I sing the wonderful hymn *'Great is Thy Faithfulness'* my spirits are lifted.

The hymn was written by Thomas Chisholm (1866 - 1960). It reminds me about God's faithfulness in a changing world and much, much more!

Often we say we have a 'deep faith' but often our faith, sadly, is dependant upon our circumstances, our moods, our emotions, our frame of mind, etc. But God's faithfulness is unfailing, unswerving, unfaltering.

I don't know the story behind this hymn but I am so grateful it was written, it must lift countless hearts as it is sung.

When the writer wrote this hymn in 1923, he probably had no idea just how popular it would become! Chisholm a teacher and ordained Methodist minister, wrote over 1,000 poems, many of which have been set to music.

23rd September

We're told in Hebrews that without faith it is impossible to please God. Many of us can recall times in our own lives when we have just had to exercise our faith while standing on the promises of God. I could most definitely write a book on the subject!

"Faith can move mountains..." we say (a reference to the words of Jesus).

Jesus speaks so much about 'faith.'

You can't read very far into the Bible without seeing faith being exercised.

Today, many people put their faith in themselves, their spouses, their parents, their children and especially, in their money. I tell you, and you already know it, every single one of these things can (will) let you down. God will never let you down.

Dear reader, I don't want you to finish reading this book without realising afresh or for the first time just how much you are loved by God. I recall the first time that I realised this in my own life and was truly amazed!

That the God of all creation should love me, moves me so deeply.

I sang it as a child... *'Jesus loves me this I know, for the Bible tells me so...'* But that was only head knowledge and a distant thought, a catchy tune etc, but years later when I knew the extent of His love for me... oh! when the head knowledge changed to heart knowledge, how it changed everything. That He would want a relationship with a wretch like me leaves me dumbstruck! I hope that you know this for yourself... how much you are loved.

So much so, that He opened His arms wide for us and died.

24th September

'Who, being loved, is poor?' Oscar Wilde.

25th September

Did you hear about the man who got to heaven and wanted answers to so many questions?

145

On arrival he decided to ask about timing.

Man: God, what exactly is a million years to you?

God: A second.

Man: And what is a million pound to you?

God: A penny.

Man: May I have a penny?

God: Wait a second.

....

26th September

'For what does it profit a man, if he shall gain the whole world, and lose his own soul?'

Mark 8:36.

....

27th September

THE CHURCH MAGAZINE

I've just read it now in the Church magazine
A poser for kids... of all ages
To select from the Bible, a character
And then write a rhyme for its pages.

As if it's not hard enough, rhyming up words
Without turning it into an ordeal!
For there's hundreds of folk in the Bible
Who deserve a due mention I feel.

The characters can represent us
They can help us, whatever our fear
Whenever trial or sorrow besets us
We can to these characters refer.

Who hasn't? Ask I, felt like Thomas?

Who can't share in his joy, when he KNEW
How good to have earnest reservations
And to carry out seeking, right through.

There is Ruth, with such love for her kin
A Moabite whom God chose to bless
(Could you love your ma-in-law like that?
… but this is no place to confess!)

And Esther, she salvaged God's people
Her year long preparation, some surprise
She felt the 'burden' upon her
From her dear uncle Mordecai's cries.

And Mary!! What strength! No words to describe
Imagine an Angel, down from above
Without struggle she surrendered as 'handmaiden'
Her motive founded only on love.

Then Joseph too, a man among men
Who believed without question or shame
Accepted their fate and position
No accusations, no queries, no blame.

Who hasn't, like Peter, failed the Lord?
Not just once did he let the side down
Apart from denying his Master
His lack of faith nearly caused him to drown.

And isn't that just what happens to us?
Our eyes are distracted by things
Instead we should keep them on Jesus
And we'll share in the Peace this then brings.

147

The list is just endless! Wide ranging.
How can I possibly choose one from them all?
And who reading this as a believer,
can deny that they've not heard the call?

The call from the central main character,
from the beginning to end He is there.
Whose words challenge and counsel us,
whose love casteth out all our fear.

He's there! Throughout God's own plan,
He's with you and me at this time
He's coming again and in Glory,
and that's the end of this rhyme.

Jackie Doherty.

28th September

29th September

Who of us, Christian or not, could not be moved by the beautiful words attributed to Mother Teresa:

'Spread love everywhere you go: first of all in your own house.

Give love to your children, your wife or husband, to a next door neighbour...

Let no one ever come to you without leaving better and happier.

Be the living expression of God's kindness: kindness in your face, kindness in your eyes, kindness in your smile, kindness in your warm greeting.'

These wise words transcend all peoples, all races, all creeds, all religions.

30th September

Mother Teresa born Agnese Gonxhe Bojaxhiu, (1910 - 1997), an Albanian, Roman Catholic nun with Indian Citizenship, was a peace maker, winning the Nobel Peace Prize in 1979.

Following her death she was Beatified by the late Pope John Paul II and had the title Blessed Teresa of Calcutta bestowed upon her.

Mother Teresa first felt the 'call' at the age of twelve, and in 1946 on September 10th she felt her second calling, or 'the call within the call' as she described it.

There is just so much to read and know about her life that I could not do it justice in a few short paragraphs. Latterly it has come to light that she suffered great doubt and often felt far from God, even in the work that she undertook in His name and for His people. I find this fact most encouraging and indeed it echoes the same doubts and fears that many of the 'great' people of God also feel, we know, don't we, as believers that it is only when we are out on a limb, so to speak, for God that we can often experience these times, and can easily understand the reason for it!! We only have to read Job to get a clearer understanding!!

I know of no other person, this century, who has done more for the poor, the lonely, the dying, the unloved than this little person, who battled with ill health on several levels, battled with doubts and was even criticised by some people! She never defended herself and that reminds me of Christ so much. I had the great privilege once to meet someone who was raised in one of her orphanages and who spoke so knowingly of her.

When first she felt the 'call' she never could have known how God was going to use her, to show His love in the world.

OCTOBER

1st October

'A smile… is a curve… that can straighten many things.'

2nd October

3rd October

'Jesus said, "Look at the birds of the air; they do not sow or reap or store away in barns, and yet your heavenly Father feeds them. Are you not much more valuable than they?"' Matthew 6: 26.

....

4th October

HARVEST GIFTS

We all know the word of ' Harvest' and the traditions that always abound
We're well used to the decorating and the laying numerous 'gifts' all around
We all pause to reflect on God's beauty, to recall Harvest Festivals past
We even sing some special songs and bring gifts that may never last.

We thank God, I suppose, in this manner, for the beauty of life He's supplied
But more than an outward appearance, we must praise Him from deep down inside.
And yes! We can 'lay up' our gifts, not just the apples, potatoes or the bread
For greater than these gifts we offer, we must offer our lives up instead.

For each of us all, has a 'gift'. To be used here and there in each place
And to hide our gifts from each other… and God, is really a shame… a disgrace.
You may think that there's nothing you have that God could possibly use
A feeling of total inadequacy, but it's really a feeble excuse.

Some people do have 'special' gifts, of course, we all know that's true
What then is to become of we humbler folk? I say there is much more we could do!
Our lives are a gift God gave to us, How we use it, is our gift to Him.
Let's not worry then about what to 'lay up'. Simply open our hearts from within.

It doesn't matter what we bring in our boxes, it's in our hearts, that God wants to see
An overflowing barrow of veggies' worth less than a humble heart, we'd agree!
A mother can devote her whole life to God, in her care for the family and home
With love and compassion and neighbourliness, so needed, when others feel so alone.

A soldier can offer his life to God, to serve, to trust, to obey.
To maintain peace and stability, yet, when needs must, rise to fight all the way.
A father can offer so many things, not least his very own soul
And God in return will Bless them, empowering their lives as a whole.

A child can offer their simple faith, indeed, we can all do the same.
By leaning on God for our guidance and trusting in His special name.

From the Harvest of our hearts then
We must offer and share all our gifts
Above and beyond the Harvest theme
Nurturing love and growth… not rifts.

And so friends… at this very Harvest time
In our thanks and our offerings
Let's praise God our creator
And feel the joy… that shared worship brings.

Jackie Doherty 11/10/89

5th October

6th October

Can you remember Harvest Festivals at school or at church when you were young?

I have wonderful happy memories of both, and then later on, going to Harvest Suppers which helped bring communities together and raised money for good causes.

Sadly, in many areas of the UK, there is no Harvest celebration any more! When we lived in Holland and Germany quite recently, there was always evidence of Autumn and Harvest celebration. Most homes put an autumn garland on their door! Many others put out gourds and squashes on their front steps and gardens, it is a wonderful reminder of God's Provision.

Special songs used to be sung also on a Harvest theme:

'Come. Ye Thankful People Come.' was one of those favourite songs, it was written by Henry Alford (1810 - 1871) who came from five generations, (a long line) of believers.

The young Henry was a child prodigy and was writing from the age of six, when he wrote and illustrated 'The Travels of St Paul.'

He was a churchman, true scholar, copious poet, writer, theologian and artist.

Just reading about his life is so inspiring!

I can't help wondering if he ever imagined when writing this hymn, that it would be used year in year out, in the worship of the church down the centuries!

The words appear simple but have a profound meaning and message, it begins with the present Harvest and ends with that Final Harvest, when God will gather all His people to Him: *'free from sorrow, free from sin.'*

7th October

When I was little, each Harvest Festival time at our Church, mum would send us off, the three of us, my two brothers and me. With a varied assortment of 'gifts', my mum and dad never came to church with us. (My dad was Jewish and my mum for various, reasons stopped attending church, I write more about this in my book *'Pete Doherty, My Prodigal Son'*.) However, mum ensured that we three children attended church and Sunday School every week without fail!

As my brothers got older they didn't like going to church or Sunday School and would set off each week with me. We'd be dressed to the nines, me with my ringlets, hat and gloves and my poor brothers with a quiff in place, the quiff was produced by having sugar water on their hair and then a metal contraption called a waver, used to hold the hair in place (believe me it was fashionable at the time!!)

Off we would go with money for the collection… however, once we got to the top of our road, both brothers would head off to the bus stop and jump on a number nineteen to the Pier Head! They always arrived back in time not to arouse suspicion and of course I was threatened not to 'snitch' or else. I never knew what 'or else' actually was, but had a good imagination. I remember them doing this on a Harvest Festival Sunday and getting caught out, not before they'd enjoyed their usual trip though with a banquet of fruit thrown in.

Mixed Blessings

8th October

'If you see someone without a smile today...

Give them one of yours...

They'll probably give it right back again!!'

9th October

The visiting preacher was on his way to a country church, in the middle of nowhere, in his old car, when, after a bumpy ride the car decided to call it a day!

As he waited by the side of the car, thinking what to do next, a cow came across the field to near where he was and said to the preacher:

'My, that sounds like your head gasket is going!'

Amazed, the preacher didn't quite know what to make of it, when a farmer came by, on the way to church for the Harvest Festival.

The preacher asked him if he owned the said field of cows and went on to report what had transpired between the cow and himself not three minutes since.

The farmer rubbed his head,

'Was it that black and white cow there?' he asked.

'Why, yes it was!' exclaimed the preacher.

'Ah, that be Ginny, you oughtn't to believe anything she says! She knows nothing about motor cars!'

10th October

'Don't be deceived: God cannot be mocked. A man reaps what he sows. The one who sows to please his sinful nature, from that nature will reap destruction; the one who sows to please the Spirit, from the Spirit will reap eternal life.'

Galatians 6:7-8.

156

11th October

AS YE SOW

As ye sow, so shall ye reap
Warning words that touch us deep
Help us then these lessons keep … in the darkest hours

Those who sow in tears will reap with songs of joy
A promise, from the Psalms, to stand on and employ.
God's love for us, the enemy cannot destroy... not even in the darkest hours.

Jackie Doherty

··

12th October

WHY DID THE SHEEP CROSS THE ROAD?

TO GET TO THE BABA'S SHOP FOR A HAIRCUT!!

··

13th October

Who hasn't heard of the famous London *'Pearly King and Queens?'* My husband is a Londoner, not in the true cockney fashion of course, because he wasn't born within the sound of 'Bow Bells' but a Londoner none the less and so, I have always hoped that he would be able to show me the infamous Pearlies, almost thirty four years later I am still waiting!!

I have seen them in films and in books and adore their costumes, many of which have been handed down.

The tradition of the Pearly King and Queens was all started by an orphan around 1875 called Henry Croft (1862 - 1930). Henry started out as a road sweeper / rat catcher, it's written that he was a small man standing about five foot. The Pearly motto is: *'ONE NEVER KNOWS.'* Henry was the first pearly King and today, I believe there are 28 Pearly King and Queen families in London, one for each of the boroughs.

It all came about because Henry wanted to give some money to the 'home' he was brought up in and had noticed among the stall holders that he befriended, that the Costers as they were known, stitched pearly buttons on their trousers to set them apart from the other traders. Henry also noticed how well these people cared for each other.

He decided to sew pearl buttons all over his clothes to try and raise money for people worse off.

The London Pearly King and Queen Society is still going strong. It is a registered charity and still raise enormous funds today for charitable causes.

Henry began something that raises money, brings cheer to people's hearts and has stood the test of time.

As he sowed on those first buttons well over a hundred years ago he could never have known that generations to come would continue the good works and that people all over the world would be fascinated by the costumes and that as a result money would be raised for good causes.

....

14th October

My eldest daughter was home recently and she loves to make ginger tea, using fresh ginger. I was watching her and was trying hard not to interfere; she's a grown up! She is perfectly able to make, her own, exotic teas, without me chipping in with advice!!

After a few days and having her alongside me in the kitchen I also observed her using garlic for a recipe and again wanted to impart some of my knowledge! Ha! What is it about mothers? We always have to say something!

Sometime later we were discussing suffering and different aspects of it that people seem to go through and I immediately thought of her in the kitchen with the ginger and the garlic and shared my analogy with her as seemed appropriate.

When using ginger, garlic, grapes for wine, it is better, if not important that they be crushed well first, this brings out the full flavour. Yes you can cut up a bit of ginger, put it in a cup and pour boiling water to infuse it, but if you crush it first you can produce a stronger, richer flavour, borne out of the crushing, likewise for garlic and wine and many other culinary items.

So it is often for us, sometimes we are crushed spiritually and every other way too and out of that crushing, comes, a stronger, more powerful person.

That which doesn't kill us makes us stronger.

15th October

'How beautiful is youth! How bright it gleams
With it's illusions, aspirations, dreams.'

Longfellow.

16th October

Can't men be awkward though?

You ask:	Darling, would you like some coffee?
They say:	No, tea please.
You ask later:	Would you like a nightcap of Whisky?
They say:	No, Brandy.
The following day enquire:	Would you like tea with breakfast?
They say:	No, coffee.
You ask:	How would you like your eggs?
They say:	One fried, one scrambled.
You ask:	Did you enjoy your breakfast?
They say:	No! You scrambled the wrong egg!

Sometimes you can't win!

17th October

'Come near to God and he will come near to you.'

James 4:8.

18th October

CRUSHED

Crushed but not broken
Down but not out
Trusting in Him
With never a doubt

Believing He's with me
Through thick and thin
Refreshing, restoring
Without and within.

Jackie Doherty

19th October

20th October

Who cannot know, at least, the name, of that great Renaissance artist, painter, sculptor, engineer, architect and poet Michaelangelo?

Born in Italy as Michaelangelo di Lodovici Buanarroti Simoni (1475 - 1564).

At the time of writing, I have never been to the Sistine Chapel where perhaps his most famous works can be seen. Scenes from Genesis and The Last Judgement can be seen, I believe, on the altar wall.

The ceiling is just something else, depicting many famous scenes inspired by the Bible such as the creation of Adam, Adam and Eve in the Garden of Eden, The Great Flood and Isaiah. The ceiling took four years to complete. Michaelangelo was always working on something and was a driven man. Often he wouldn't eat or drink and never bothered about his personal appearance nor gave concern over money, it was always his work. At just the age of 24 he sculpted the famous Pieta, a most beautiful piece depicting Jesus on His mother's lap following His crucifixion.

This inspired artist has brought such joy, pleasure, beauty, understanding and insight to countless numbers of people through the work of his hands, his mind and his passion. We may never know what drove and encouraged him, he could never have known that his work would still be cherished, admired and loved, 500 hundred years later, by all people of all faiths.

21st October

When we read, see or hear of those great artists, musicians, writers it could leave us feeling rather deflated. "What on earth can I do?" We may ask ourselves. You may have your own answers but for my part, whilst I can't even draw a straight line nor sing, not to mention play a musical note nor would I call what I do with my pen 'writing' in the true sense of the word, I do what I can, where and when I am able.

We must never look to another person and in that looking demean ourselves, that is not how God wants our hearts to be. We are all a part of the body, yes in medicine, we call some body parts 'vital' parts and still, they are only a part of the whole body.

I have learned (and often relearned!) many things in my time and one thing that I have grasped and understood for my own life is that we must 'do' whatever it is that we do 'do' for the glory of God. Whether that be in our housework, in our cooking, in our ironing. (Just yesterday, I overheard two young woman saying how much they hated ironing! Years ago when the children were little and there was always laundry, I would begin my ironing in prayer and each piece that I ironed I would pray for the child or person to whom it belonged, it became a labour of love indeed - I miss it today) in our serving our neighbour, our families, our co workers. God sees our heart attitude in these things and will use our 'little' things greatly, not perhaps for world renown or even gratitude, but you can be sure that every single thing that we do for Him is seen.

22nd October

'Why worry... when you can pray!'

....

23rd October

The farmer had been standing in his field when the doctor had passed that way some two hours before. The doctor thought it rather strange but carried on about his duties. At the end of his working day and driving past the farm again the doctor noticed that Ben the farmer was still stood standing in the field!

It was almost dark now and the doctor thought it best to check if there was anything the matter as he was himself intrigued!

'Hi, Ben, saw you there before and earlier today, is everything alright?'

'Oh, Yes, thanks doc, all's good, I'm hoping for a Nobel Prize!'

Thinking the farmer had cracked the doctor continued 'A Nobel Prize!? Why then are you here?'

'I read that Nobel Prizes were awarded to those outstandin' in their field!'

....

24th October

The Sheep and The Goats

'"When the Son of Man comes in His glory, and all the angels with him, he will sit on his throne in heavenly glory. All the nations will be gathered before him and he will separate the people one from another as a shepherd separates the sheep from the goats.

He will put the sheep on his right and the goats on his left. Then the King will say to those on his right, 'Come you who are blessed by my Father; take your inheritance, the kingdom prepared for you since the creation of the world. For I was hungry and you gave me something to eat, I was thirsty and you gave me something to drink, I was a stranger and you invited me in, I needed clothes and you clothed me, I was sick and you looked after me, I was in prison and you came to visit me.

Then the righteous will answer him, 'Lord, when did we see you hungry and feed you, or thirsty and give you something to drink? When did we see you a stranger and invite you in, or needing clothes and clothe you? When did we see you sick or in prison and go to visit you?'

The King will reply, 'I tell you the truth, whatever you did for one of the least of these brothers of mine, you did for me.'

Then he will say to those on his left, 'Depart from me, you who are cursed, into the eternal fire prepared for the devil and his angels. For I was hungry and you did not feed me, I was thirsty and you gave me nothing to drink, I was a stranger and you did not invite me in, I needed clothes and you did not clothe me, I was sick and in prison and you did not look after me.'

They will also answer, 'Lord, when did we see you hungry or thirsty or a stranger or needing clothes or sick or in prison, and we did not help you?'

He will reply, 'I tell you the truth, whatever you did not do for one of the least of these, you did not do for me.'

Then they will go away to eternal punishment, but the righteous to eternal life.'" Jesus teaching in Matthew 25 v 31- 46.

···

25th October

SHOW ME.

> *Show me today how I may help*
> *Show me today whom I may help*
> *Show me today where I may help*
> *Show me*
> *Today.*

Jackie Doherty.

···

26th October

The Vicarage — Oh! my goodness you're telling me about the family at number 10! The mother is in hospital, the seven children are cold and hungry and about to be evicted, the father has run off - - - - Can I ask who you are dear fellow?

I'm the Landlord!

163

27th October

There may be a few of you, dear readers who have heard of William Willett, but this month all of you will be carrying out a procedure that he instigated almost a hundred years ago!

It will be time once again to put the clocks back:

William Willett was an English builder who was passionate about saving daylight time and eventually, using his own money, he published a paper entitled 'The waste of daylight.' Even a young Winston Churchill liked the idea. Willett wasn't the first to be concerned about conserving daylight, Benjamin Franklin often spoke about such a thing. When it became Law in the UK in 1916 Germany had already introduced the scheme. Sadly William Willett died the year before the Law came into being but he left behind a legacy that affects us all.

The clocks go forward one hour at 0200 hrs on the last Sunday in March.

The clocks go back one hour at 0200hrs on the last Sunday in October.

Spring forward

Fall back.

28th October

If only I'd known that little phrase when I was younger.

I just know that I'm not going to get this story right, but bear with me!

If you knew me personally then you'd know that I like to keep good time, in fact, I am usually early, too early, for everything! But I remember with fondness a story from my teenage years.

I had a lunch date with a young man and was quite excited about it, plus I was hungry! As usual I was ready way ahead of time and sat down in the chair to wait, when I heard the radio ask if we'd remembered to change the clocks. In a panic about not knowing the true time and not knowing whether it was to have been back or forward the clock should be, I waited and waited for the radio to give the correct time... and in the waiting fell to sleep!

Having made a nice young man wait and wait for almost two hours, I missed lunch and I missed a nice date, even though he'd waited, he then had to go to work!

Talk about all dressed up and nowhere to go...

29th October

'Better late than never

But better never late.'

30th October

I like the joke about poor Harry who was always in trouble for being late for work. Try as he may, even using three alarm clocks, he was often late and had been warned by his understanding boss, who suggested Harry should consult his doctor about it.

Wanting to please his boss, Harry went straight to the doctor's after work and the doctor prescribed him a pill that would do the trick! Before retiring Harry took the pill and lo and behold he woke up bright as a button two hours before the first alarm clock!

Harry was pleased and got into work before his boss and couldn't wait to tell him the news 'I went straight to the Docs and took the pill and was awake two hours before the first alarm clock, I feel great!' The boss had a scowl on his face and it made Harry uneasy and he asked 'What's the matter, boss?'

The boss scratched his head and said 'Well, that's great Harry! But where were you yesterday!'

31st October

'He has showed you, O man, what is good,
And what does the Lord require of you?
To act justly and to love mercy and to walk humbly with your God.'
Micah 6:8.

Mixed
Blessings

1st November

NOVEMBER

November's here, the days grow dark
The leaves lay deep within the park
The nights arrive in the afternoon
And autumn's fading all too soon...

Yet what a wonder filled time it brings
A time for comforting, leisurely things
Of home made soups and an open fire
Of jigsaw puzzles in night attire

Of gently lit rooms and flannelette sheets
Of window shopping in neon lit streets
Of mentally planning for Christmas beyond
Though knowing it's far too soon to respond

Of coming indoors, when the chill's in the air
Collapsing dog tired in the favourite chair
Of knowing all nature is slowing its pace
And settling down in its seasonal place.

November's a time that fills hearts with cheer
The penultimate month of a very long year
So, although it's cold and the North wind doth blow
There's a promise of rebirth in the rain and the snow.

Jackie Doherty.

2nd November

....

3rd November

Whenever I see a Salvation Army member selling the WAR CRY or hear their band playing I am moved to pray for the work that they do in God's name, feeding the poor, befriending the lonely, helping the underprivileged up and down the country and across international countries.

In my heart I see these people as very much doing as Christ impelled, to stretch out our hands to the poor and needy. They fill my heart with admiration and respect and I cannot pass either without thanking God for their witness and their love and as a fellow believer feel duty (love) bound to pray for them as a whole and individually. Of course the individuals are like you and me, mere mortals, humans who face daily temptations and disappointments. They are to be commended for trying to make a difference in this world, a world that hasn't changed very much since the founder of The Salvation Army first began this great work among the poor and needy of London's streets.

William Booth (1829 - 1912) was born in Nottingham and from age thirteen was an apprentice in a Pawnbrokers shop (eventually moving to London) which enabled him to support his family. He became a Christian in his early teens, some records say this was at age fifteen. Through his work he often met with people who had fallen on hard times, ill health, alcoholism, crime, homelessness, prostitution, and was very moved by this, knowing that faith in Jesus would help them. He became a Methodist minister and would often preach in the streets.

In 1865 he was preaching outside the Blind Beggar Pub in the East End of London when a group of missioners heard him and invited Booth to lead some open air meetings and from this he formed his own movement called the Christian Mission which eventually changed to The Salvation Army in 1878, which grew rapidly. At the end of Booth's life, The Sally Army as it is lovingly called in Liverpool, was operational in 58 countries!

Their mission statement:

Today it is an International movement, an evangelical part of the universal Christian Church. Its mission is to preach the gospel of Jesus Christ and to meet human needs in His name without discrimination.

General William Booth didn't have an 'easy' time of it, he was criticised by many, including Christians, made fun of in public, but he followed through on what he believed was his mission, by the grace of God.

As a young man he could never have believed how his work would continue into the 21st Century, Kings and Queens, parliaments, social plans have come and gone but still, all over the world, not just in Britain, there is such a need for the work of the Salvation Army, we still have the poor, the needy, the sick, the lonely, alcohol and drug addicts, criminals, prostitutes, homelessness in our midst.

I have met people who have been helped by The Salvation Army, whose lives have been turned around. General Booth may have died over 100 years ago but his legacy lives on.

4th November

The Blind Beggar pub in Whitechapel, is very much alive and kicking in the East End of London and there has been a pub/inn on that site for centuries. It is a popular tourist attraction for many and not least for Salvationists, who know, that that is where William Booth preached, there is a statue of him nearby. I, too, know of the Blind Beggar Pub because my son lived in that area several times over several years, first as a student at the age of nineteen.

It seemingly is so called because of a legend long believed about a Henry de Montfort (son of Simon) who lost his sight in battle in the thirteenth century and became known as the Blind Beggar of Bethnal Green and was immortalised and popularised by Percy in his poetical writings of the 18th Century.

There is a Besse street nearby and this is attributed to Henry's daughter Besse. Of course, the pub has other strong connections with the Kray Twins, dating back to the last century, who were renowned East End gangsters.

5th November

'Please do remember the fifth of November

Gunpowder treason and plot...'

6th November

I served with the Queen Alexandra's Royal Army Nursing Corps for six years and can remember when there was still a 'Pay Parade'. This was the process of receiving one's pay from the Army and involved standing in formation on parade until your name was called and then you would stand to attention and say after checking your pay, 'Pay and pay book correct, Sir!' before saluting and leaving the 'Parade.'

I only attended a few of these parades before having my pay paid into my bank account but can remember being petrified of making a mistake during the lengthy process.

There was always a story to be told regarding Pay Parades and I would laugh at them all, the one I love which I was told was true (!) is about a new recruit who was on such a Parade being held in the company office, in those days one had to sign on a pay roll with several carbon copies before receiving pay.

Apparently the young recruit had signed so lightly that it hadn't gone through the copies, so the paymaster bellowed: 'Put your weight on it laddie!'

Obedient to the last, the recruit bent forward and wrote beside his name - Ten Stone.

7th November

The Lord's Prayer

Our Father which art in Heaven,
hallowed be thy name.
Thy kingdom come,
thy will be done on earth as it is in heaven.
Give us this day our daily bread and forgive us our trespasses
as we forgive those who trespass against us
and lead us not into temptation but deliver us from evil.
For thine is the kingdom the power and the glory for ever and ever.

Amen

8th November

GOOD MORNING

Our Father, be with me today
In all I do, in all I say
Open my eyes in every way
And hear me Father as I pray.

I bring to you my heart of sin
That judges, criticises... out and in
I bring my mind and the thoughts therein
I pray you hear as I begin...

Use my life today for You
For people ... You would bring me to
Grant grace and strength to see me through
In all the deeds You bid me do.

Forgive me for the sins committed
The ones I've made and ones omitted
The ones on purpose, those unwitted
Free my heart from pain embittered

Whatever comes my way this day
As clothed am I, in a spiritual way
With all of the Armour you display
Protect me, Father, this I pray.

Jackie Doherty.

9th November

WHY DID THE RABBIT CROSS THE ROAD ?

TO GET TO THE... HOPPING MALL !!

10th November

Over the pages of this book I have mentioned very famous people, writers, hymn writers, artists, inventors alike, all of whom have inspired and encouraged me personally. It would be amiss of me not to mention something that I read every single day, it encourages me to read my Bible each day and I have been using it since 1982. As soon as I wake up, before the kettle is on, even before I brush my teeth I pick up my copy of *'Our Daily Bread'* and within five minutes my heart is set on the things of God, already within those five minutes I have read a portion of scripture and my mind is lifted beyond the mundane. Later in the day I make further time for other things, on different days I attend Bible studies and fellowship groups and the like, but the early morning time, set aside in this manner has been the basis of my daily relationship with God.

I cannot stress how often I have felt that the articles had just been written for me!! My children and wider family know and love my booklets and often get a spare copy when I have one. I usually carry my spare copies ready to prayerfully give them away as the Spirit leads.

'Our Daily Bread' is just a small (large) part of what RBC Ministries are about. Radio Bible Class Ministries work out of and for many overseas countries, they provide literature in a multiplicity of languages for ordinary people.

The booklets last three months and are totally free. There is no commitment to send money even though they are not funded or endowed by any group or denomination, support is only from gifts. In all the time that I have received 'Our Daily Bread' booklets not once have I been asked to send money. This speaks volumes to me.

I am truly grateful and indebted to 'them' and their faithful team of writers who make up 'Our Daily Bread' and so often have wanted to put pen to paper to thank each of them.

As it happens I never have a spare copy for long!

I was at a gig of my son's some years ago now, at the Hackney Empire and as I was leaving a fan of his told me that she and her group of friends were Christians and that they were praying for him and the family and then amazed me by saying that she'd even given him a copy of 'Our Daily Bread'!

When I have been speaking in prisons in the past, RBC Ministries have provided me with various books to take with me. Prisoners have told me that they enjoy reading 'Our Daily Bread' booklets and other literature. It speaks to your heart.

You can write to them for your copy or for a copy for a friend :

RBC Ministries, PO Box 1, Carnforth, Lancs LA5 9ES. England.

Their bookmark encourages me to : Apply the scripture passage to my life, to ask myself: What does it teach about God's character? My relationship with Him? With others? Dangers to avoid? Promises to embrace.

11th November

Remembrance Day.

Even though I have no favourite writers among the Our Daily Bread team (they are all favourites!) each writer has their own unique style, sometimes I can recognise a writer almost before the first paragraph is read, there is only the one writer whom I have had the privilege to meet. Sadly, she is no longer living, a gifted writer and speaker called Joanie Yoder, author of many books but a favourite of mine is 'The God dependant Life'. I have had the pleasure of meeting and hearing Joanie Yoder speak twice.

She spoke of many things during those two meetings and much of it I have retained but amazingly she spoke over and over about her love for drug addicts and how she and her husband Bill opened their home to some. (Bill sadly passed away some years before Joanie.) Why this had stuck with me I could never have known, maybe God was preparing my heart for what was to come.

12th November

'We never know what tomorrow brings.'

13th November

Can you imagine how Robinson Crusoe felt when he found a footprint in the sand? He must have felt that at last his lonely existence was brought to an end.

It didn't matter to him who had made the footprint as long as the owner was friendly, it was more to do with someone, anyone, just being there.

We often see people on their own lonely island and feel unable to take the small step necessary to help them feel less isolated in this busy world. Often a smile, a wave or a kind word can make all the difference.

We should make 'impressions' like this on any day of the week… we don't have to wait for a Friday!

14th November

'Do to others as you would have them do to you.'

Spoken by Jesus in Luke 6:31.

15th November

WHAT'S THIS?

> *What's this I read within the verse?*
> *That makes me want to turn away*
> *The very thought's to me, perverse*
> *But, to 'love' my enemies, is His way.*

Now let me check I've got it right
I'm to do good to those who hate me!
To bless those who curse me too
And pray for those who ill treat me!

Now that's a mind set hard to grasp
It takes a heart filled with His love
And we could never reach those heights
Without the help of God above...

Jackie Doherty

16th November

Church Notice Board

Don't let your worries
Kill you...
why not let the
Church help!
ring *ernvm* today.

17th November

Probably most famous today for his hymn *'All Glory Laud and Honour'* Theodulph of Orleans (760 - 821) wrote many works of poetry and prose, he was a scholar and became Bishop of Orleans. It is believed that he wrote the now famous hymn whilst imprisoned in Angier.

He experienced much trouble and controversy in his life and was imprisoned for no good reason for several years in the latter part of his life.

His words written nearly 12 centuries ago have brought inspiration to countless numbers of people down the ages, he could never have known at the time of writing just how long his hymn would last.

18th November

CHILDREN LEARN WHAT THEY LIVE

If a child lives with criticism... he learns to condemn.
If a child lives with hostility... he learns to fight.
If a child lives with ridicule... he learns to be shy.
If a child lives with shame... he learns to feel guilty.
If a child lives with tolerance... he learns to be patient.
If a child lives with encouragement... he learns confidence.
If a child lives with praise... he learns to appreciate.
If a child lives with fairness... he learns justice.
If a child lives with security... he learns to have faith.
If a child lives with approval... he learns to like himself.
If a child lives with acceptance and friendship...
... he learns to find LOVE in the world.

19th November

Someone once told me that to achieve happiness, married couples should resemble a pair of garden shears - joined together so they cannot be separated, working for one aim, though often moving in opposite directions, yet always coming together to remove anything coming between them.

20th November

WHY DO GOLFERS ALWAYS CARRY A SPARE PAIR OF SOCKS WHEN THEY PLAY?

IN CASE THEY GET A HOLE IN ONE!

21st November

'So do not fear, for I am with you; do not be dismayed for I am your God. I will strengthen you and help you: I will uphold you with my righteous right hand.'

Isaiah 41:10

22nd November

I found this ditty recently which I wrote in 1980

NO GENTLE CHAT

I've never had green fingers but didn't think it hard
To pot and plant young seedlings, but now I'm really on my guard.

I've been married now for four years and that adds up to many days
And I must have lost as many plants in as many different ways.

Baby bio, rooting powder, loving care, I've tried in vain
Dark corners or bright sunlight, even standing in the rain

And still they seem to die off leaving me a sorry show
When I look at other peoples plants I ask them all they know!

Then hurry back to my house and practise all I've learned
And wait to see a seedling grow, surely a plant I've earned

But no! no matter my plan of action what strategies I ply
The leaves still turn to yellow and the darned things start to die.

I've coddled them, caressed them, I've talked until I'm green
I've spent a little fortune, still no decent plant I've seen.

Until last week I met a gem, a lady of many years
Confided in me her secret touch and whispered in my ears.

The very next morn, I ran downstairs, having put the plan apace
You could hardly see my living room for the plants about the place.

So, for all you budding 'planters' who would like to know the score
On how to get your plants to grow, listen in... I'll tell you more

You can forget the gentle chatting and your money you can stow
Just threaten them ... that you'll sing to them! Then sit back and watch 'em grow!

Jackie Doherty.

23rd November

24th November

Walk down any city high street and very quickly you will see evidence of homelessness and hardship as seen in the selling of the *'Big Issue.'*

When possible, I always take time these days, to chat with the sellers who often through no fault of their own have become homeless and usually have a multiplicity of problems, which they seem to be addressing with help, I have noticed how upbeat, polite and cheerful most sellers are and it is always a pleasure to spend time in their company.

Many years ago I would have found it difficult to stop and talk, probably because my heart, without me even knowing it, was full of criticism and I was being judgmental. God has dealt with me in this area, (and many other areas too!) mainly through reading and focusing on the Parable of the Prodigal Son.

I could surely write a book about this parable and all it has taught me... and continues to teach me.

Do you have a prodigal in the family, dear reader? Maybe you are a prodigal.

In a nutshell that barely does it justice, I discovered, my heart discovered, that each of us at some point in our lives, is one of the lead parts of this parable! The errant son, or the son at home, but living in defeat, even the role of the waiting loving father, (there is no mention of a mother!) I commend this parable to you, read it, pray about it, ask God, by His Holy Spirit to reveal truths you may have missed before.

Out of the blue, four years ago now, I was invited to write a piece for the *'Big Issue'* for one of their light hearted features entitled *'Queen for a Day'* ('King' if you're a male!) which I thoroughly enjoyed and reminded me so clearly of that beautiful Bible verse *'And we know that all things work together for good to those who love God, who are called according to His purpose.'* Romans 8:28.

25th November

Something which always strikes me whenever I see a *'Big Issue'* seller is their confidence. They seem to be very confident, I shudder to think how many of us would be able to cope as hundreds of people pass by without making eye contact, acting as though the seller didn't exist.

I understand only too well the issue of confidence.

On the surface, most people would describe me as a confident person, certainly I had never experienced any confidence issues. That was until a few years back when I would read and see things in the papers or on-line about me or members of my family, written by people who didn't know me, words written in black and in white which were completely untrue! Throughout my life I have always loved the Psalms and I recall reading them and often could apply them to my own life. Whenever I read about people telling lies I would be wondering why the Psalmist would write that and for me I would think it impossible that people would lie about me or my family. But goodness me how I have learned from this and gained strength from the Psalms knowing that I must 'love' those who hurt me and that vengeance is not mine!

There were days when I would find it very difficult to leave the house, to go to work, to talk with my neighbours, I couldn't 'sue' anyone as I would never be out of court, nor did I wish to enter into that arena. A dear friend reminded me that I should pray for the very people that had written the articles!!!

She was right of course. I couldn't run around the world and protest the truth, my nanny used to say that *'a lie would travel the earth whilst truth was putting on her boots'* (taken from Mark Twain, I think) I never understood this as a child but do now as an adult, sadly!

But I did leave the house, I did go to work and yes! I even talked with my neighbours not because of anything in me, but because of everything in Him, I was able to put on my lipstick, hold my head high and walk through the raging storm.

'In quietness and confidence shall be your strength'

Isaiah 30:15.

Are you in the middle of a storm, dear reader?

Do you know that you are so precious to God.

He is so much bigger than anything you can be going through, give it to Him today.

You have nothing to lose and everything to gain.

26th November

'Blessed is the man who trusts in the Lord, whose confidence is in Him.

He will be like a tree planted by the water that sends out its roots by the stream.

It does not fear when heat comes; its leaves are always green.

It has no worries in a year of drought and never fails to bear fruit.'

Jeremiah 17:7- 8.

27th November

'That old law about an 'eye for an eye' leaves everybody blind!' Martin Luther King.

28th November

'I rejoice therefore that I have confidence in you in all things.'
2 Corinthians 7:16.

29th November

CONFIDENCE

How can I put on this lipstick! How can I walk through the door?
How can I chat with my neighbours with whom I've chatted before?

Why is my heart all a tremble! Why is my spirit cast down?
Why can't I just lift my head up! Why is my smile now a frown?

I'll bring it to God straightaway, in prayer, in faith, in this hour
My part is only to call Him, then to trust upon His healing power.

Jackie Doherty.

30th November

1st December

Here we are already! It's December and there's anticipation in the air…

The shops are gearing up for the festive frenzy, the church is busy too, it's Advent, a time of expectancy. We tend to think this is where it all began, with the babe in the manger, but that isn't strictly true, the promise and being of Christ is found all over the Old Testament.

Over the weeks, throughout this book, it has been the custom to mention books, art, inventions, songs, poetry, writers etc, that have inspired or encouraged me personally over the years. I can't let this book end without referring to the greatest inspiration, hope giver, encourager of them all… the Bible.

I remember, only too clearly, in 1982 saying to a Padre (army chaplain) 'You're not telling me that you can read the Bible and not find it boring?'

His kind, gentle, no doubt prayerful response, was to give me a copy of The Good News Bible and he said something along the lines of 'Pray before you read it that God will bless you with His Holy Spirit that you may understand, and pray for wisdom.'

And so it was over the next few years I read and reread the Bible through, I am still reading it through Genesis to Revelation and still praying for wisdom. I am never disappointed even though some parts are difficult!

Are you reading your Bible, dear reader? When did you last pick it up? Does your mind stray when you try to read it?

I believe that the Bible is the Holy word of God, it is truth. It is a 'living' word because it speaks to your heart.

The King James Bible has 50 authors, 66 books, 1,189 chapters and 31,173 verses.

Not one of those authors could have known that they would be part of a book that would be a best seller many times over, that their God-inspired writing would change people's hearts and lives down the centuries!

No, they could never have known that... but God did.

2nd December

If you knew my family then you would understand when I say that we each like to dress in... shall I say... an unusual way!

But it is my eldest daughter who takes the biscuit in the dressing department!

She's a constant topic of conversation in the wider family as they wait in anticipation to 'see' what she's wearing! Her style is unique. Even her dad, (who doesn't notice these things, notices!) In a Christmas past, whilst we were awaiting her arrival at a German airport, my hubby remarked 'I wonder what she'll be wearing' and I replied in all innocence 'Oh, she texted me to say that she'll be smart and in a suit.'

The craft had landed and we watched as passengers came through to waiting family and the like, it was two days before Christmas and emotions were running high.

The plan was to pick her up and then pay a visit to the Dusseldorf Christmas Market. I'd told her this plan some days before and she'd told me it sounded a great idea and added that she'd be suitably dressed for the occasion, I had taken it that she would wear warm clothing, just like a mother, still worrying about a child being warm, after all she was only in her thirties and a school teacher!

We awaited her emergence from the security doors as busy people raced through, again my hubby wondered aloud 'I wonder what she'll be wearing?' I responded automatically with some pride, 'She'll be in a suit.'

Finally the doors opened - The whole airport erupted as a skinny fully bearded Father Christmas with bell in hand announced:

"Ho, ho, ho... Merry Christmas everyone!"

Well!.. She was 'suited', Santa suited.

We couldn't wait for the next visit!

3rd December

'I will honour Christmas in my heart, and try to keep it all the year.'
Charles Dickens.

4th December

You know it makes sense..!

To avoid that 'run down' feeling, look both ways before crossing the road.

5th December

'A word aptly spoken is like apples of gold in settings of silver.'
Proverbs 25:11.

6th December

NO ROOM HERE

It's so strange - I often have wondered
That for God's Son - there was no room in the inn
That He came amid basic beginnings
A place lowly and humble within.

Why! That's no place for God's Son to be born!
And it's always a puzzle as to why...
An animal's shelter should house Him
When He'd the splendour of the heavenly sky.

185

No, no room in the inn, then for Jesus
But who was bothered? Who knew who He was?
Who'd imagine His birth was significant?
Not to mention His death on the cross.

But nothing ever changes
There's no room in men's hearts still today
Life's too busy, such a rush, there's no time
To think, understand or to pray

This same Jesus can't enter man's 'Inn'
Until it is humble and lowly
And then He imparts understanding
Albeit sometimes rather slowly.

I needn't have wondered so long
It's all there in the Bible to read
That He longs to dwell inside each of us
No matter our colour or creed.

He cannot dwell in a proud heart
So humble your heart from within
Don't offer the age old reply - (this Christmas)
Sorry there's no room in this Inn.

Jackie Doherty Dec 1989.

....

7th December

WHY DID THE FARMERS WIFE CROSS THE ROAD?

TO BRING THE CHICKEN AND ALL THE
OTHER ANIMALS BACK, OF COURSE!!!

8th December

I can't wait to share my next source of inspiration with you, it's not something that I have read about in books, it's not some piece of art, it's not even something from the distant past and it most certainly isn't something or someone that is no longer living.

My next personal source of hope and encouragement is very much alive!

Our connection was the result of a God-incidence.

I had been speaking on the radio and the interviewer mentioned my book and somewhere some person had heard the interview and had resolved to buy and read it. Not knowing that I was a Christian, having read *Pete Doherty My Prodigal Son,* the reader realised that I was indeed a believer and began to pray for our situation and all the family. A little while later he made contact with me through the publishers. Since that publication I have had many hundreds of letters from readers and whilst I have answered every single letter by hand (apart from when there was no address) I have avoided making 'personal' telephone contact. However, when I received this correspondence I felt a quickening in my spirit and knew that I had to make direct contact.

The person wanted nothing from me only to offer me prayer, daily prayer.

Over the months that ensued there would be random texts to my mobile offering prayer, support and encouragement and gradually a bond grew and eventually I was invited to meet the person and his darling, gifted, blessed, wonderful wife and all those he worked with!!

I had no idea that I was being upheld in prayer by a very busy group of people, that they should even be bothered with me, a praying mother, was beyond my comprehension. I was invited to speak at his 'complex' and agreed wholeheartedly, not knowing, to where or what I was going. Of course I googled the 'complex' but still had no idea what to expect.

What a 'complex'! it's the Caedmon Complex in Thornbury, Gloucester.

It's where NGM - New Generation Music work from. I could never do it justice in a few paragraphs, you need to google it for yourself to discover just what is going on under the headship of Ray and Nancy Goudie.

M
i
x
Blessings
d

Ray and Nancy used to be in a Christian Band called 'Heartbeat' and are now co-directors of NGM, below are listed just a few of the talents that they have, talents that they use for God and for the love of His people:

Ray	Nancy
Song writer	Public speaker
Producer	Author
Drummer	Broadcaster
Manager	Singer
Preacher/Teacher	Preacher/Teacher

Both, live by Faith, individually and corporately and in 2001 whilst hanging on to the vision they had and standing on the promises of God they received £3 million to purchase and build their present Mission and Arts centre, the Caedmon Complex.

Ray, co-wrote and produced the musical Luv Esther and is now working on a new musical and you may even have sung some of his worship songs 'Heal our Nation' 'I will speak out' and others.

Nancy, with her able team annually organise 'Spiritual Health Conferences' for women, in Preston and Bristol, which I highly recommend!

From Caedmon, courses are run for all age groups and The Inspire Arts Trust give first class instruction on the following:

Youthwork, Vocals, DJ Training, Music Technology, Studio Engineering, Dance, Video editing, Graphic Design, Socia Skills, Healthy Living, Overseas Experience.

This is just a glimpse into what Caedmon Complex can offer a young person, please look it up on the web, if you have or know a young person interested in any of the above don't hesitate to make contact with NGM for further information, they run 'Boot Camps' with a real difference too!

When Ray first made contact I had mistakenly thought his name was pronounced 'Goodie' which spoke volumes to me! ... But to me, they are indeed the 'Goodies...' in every sense.

When they set out from Scotland, all those years ago, called to a mission with a real passion for the youth of our land, they could never have known and probably will never know how far reaching their efforts will extend.

May God continue to Bless their work.

9th December

I cannot let this moment pass without sharing a little about the weekends that Nancy Goudie organises. I didn't really 'want' to go to a 'Health Weekend' never mind a *'Spiritual Health Weekend'*, I am not into pampering and all that, it's okay for others, but there has been little space for it in my own life. That all changed after attending one of these weekends! I'm booked in for next year already!

I'm becoming aware that I may even be boring many of my friends as I try to encourage them to participate! I cannot recommend them enough to you! If you are young, old or in between it doesn't matter, beg, borrow but don't steal the money to go, it is money very well spent, (and that is from someone who doesn't like to waste a penny!) save up for it, use birthday and Christmas money and if all else fails you can pay NGM monthly in advance to ease the financial strain! (details on line)

To come together in this way, to worship with hundreds of other believers from varied backgrounds and cultures, sharing with people you don't know, in a 4 star Hotel is unbelievable. The music is astounding, the preaching/teaching amazing, the prayers/praying beyond description. There is so much going on that it's impossible to relay it in a few lines.

Having not 'really' wanted to go, I can only add that I didn't want to leave!

I hope to meet you there too, dear reader!

10th December

'Christ is for life... not just for Christmas'

11th December

A father and his young son were stood looking at Tintoretto's famous painting of the Nativity.

"What I can't understand," said the boy, "Is why Jesus wasn't born in a bed... a proper bed! Not lain in a manger, after all He is God's only Son, surely something better could have been arranged?"

His smiling father explained that Joseph and Mary were on a journey at a very busy time and that there just wasn't any room in Bethlehem at that time and that they were, anyway, very poor.

"Can't have been that poor," responded the boy, "to get themselves painted by Tintoretto!"

12th December

'The angel went to her and said, "Greetings, you who are highly favoured! The Lord is with you."

Mary was greatly troubled at his words and wondered what kind of greeting this might be, but the angel said to her:

"Do not be afraid, Mary, you have found favour with God. You will be with child and give birth to a son, and you are to give him the name Jesus. He will be great and will be called the Son of the Most High, The Lord God will give Him the throne of His father David and He will reign over the house of Jacob for ever; His Kingdom will never end."

"How will this be," Mary asked the angel, "since I am a virgin?"

The angel answered "The Holy Spirit will come upon you, and overshadow you, so the Holy one to be born will be the Son of God. Even Elizabeth your relative is going to have a child in her old age, and she who is said to be barren is in her sixth month. For nothing is impossible with God."

"I am the Lords' servant," Mary answered. "May it be to me as you have said,"

Then the angel left her.'

LUKE Chapter 1:8-38.

13th December

THINK AGAIN...

Christmas is coming and with it, accidents too
To prevent so many mishaps, there's something you can do...

THINK AGAIN...
Accidents do happen, we all know this is true
But many are preventable and much depends on you.

It's going to be a 'wild' time, around Christmas and New Year
Parties, celebrations, people filled with cheer
But at these 'celebrations' it's known that things go awry
And people become careless and that's the reason why...

I'm pleading to your common sense
To take care this holiday
'Prevention is far better than cure'
Is as an adage people say...

THINK AGAIN... .
Be aware to possibilities, don't take risks, whilst having fun
And watch for others' lack of thought, keep an eye on everyone!

There'll be candles here and candles there
Smokers all around
Fairy lights and disco lights
An accident's breeding ground

THINK AGAIN... ..
People will be imbibing, having parties enjoying life
Not giving thought to 'taking care', to trouble or to strife.

And... these... these are the very moments
When accidents abound...
So, please to you... This Christmastime
Keep safe, Keep well, Keep sound...

Jackie Doherty 1999.

191

14th December

15th December

It's an amazing thing, to me anyway! That we can read in the Bible about two very different people and their reactions when visited by an angel. One was old and one was very young.

On the one hand we read that Zechariah, a priest, who was a righteous and Godly man 'was gripped with fear' and full of doubt, when the angel Gabriel appeared to him. Because he didn't believe Gabriel, he was struck dumb until after John, his son, was born.

On the other hand when Gabriel visited Mary, an ordinary, unwed, young woman, she accepted the message immediately, who would believe her? How was she to tell Joseph? No, she only said 'I am the Lord's Servant. May it be to me as you have said.'

Likewise when an angel appeared to Joseph, he believed and obeyed.

There was no 'why me?' 'why us?' between them and their response.

How different their response compared to the priest.

What would our response be? Would we recognise it for what it was... that God's hand was upon our life and to trust Him implicitly for whatever the future brought.

How is our response when 'trouble' comes (and it rarely comes alone!) do we say 'why me?' or do we say 'why not me!' If God be for us then who are we to fear.

16th December

Don't you just love Christmas?

I know I do.

All too often I hear adults, usually non believers say 'Oh! Christmas is only for children... ' I always answer 'Yes, for children of all ages!!' I understand though how their rose coloured view on life has grown yellow tinged! For many, Christmas brings much stress and worry and drags up old past hurts, many are lonely or missing loved ones, many just can't stand having the family round and finding little peace!

I know what it is like to miss loved ones around the table at this special time, I dearly miss my mum and dad, who are no longer alive, wherever we were living, they would travel to us or occasionally we would travel to them. I treasure those days even though at times it was stressful, it isn't always easy to juggle all the demands, the key is to keep a sense of perspective and a keen sense of humour helps!

We have our own traditions, as you will have too, in your family.

I often worked on Christmas Day as a nurse, sometimes my husband has been on duty elsewhere, now my own children can't always be home.

For the past few years we haven't been together as a whole family for different reasons, duty, distance, other commitments and I look forward to a time when once again all my children will gather around the Christmas table as a family. Whenever I want to burst into tears because all my children aren't together, as we gather round the table, I am quickly, very quickly, reminded that that is exactly how our Father God feels about his absent children!

How He misses us when we are not 'with' Him!

Then I turn my thoughts to the lonely, the sick, the dying, the bereaved, the prodigals who are away from the home. There was a song in my teens that went 'if you can't be with the one you love, love the one you're with' (this probably had other connotations! Perhaps, but it's a phrase I have never forgotten.) It reminds me to make the very most of what we have, with who we are and for us not to let circumstances rule us, rather for us to make the best of every circumstance good or bad.

I don't know yet, if my family will all be together this year... but that isn't the issue, the issue for me is that as a believer, every day... is Christmas Day.

17th December

'What can I give Him
    Poor as I am?
If I were a shepherd
    I would bring a lamb
If I were a wise man
    I would do my part
Yet, what I can give Him-
    Give my heart.'

Christina Georgina Rossetti 1830 - 1894
(last verse of the hymn, In the Bleak Mid-Winter.)

18th December

'The best thing to put into your Christmas cake... is your teeth!'

19th December

'"Glory to God in the highest, and on earth peace, good will toward men."' Luke 2:14

20th December

CHRISTMAS TREE OR XMAS TREE

There it stands…
A feast for little eyes
A symbol of what Christmas means
The glamour and surprise
The shiny, glistening baubles
The tinsel trailing round
The smell of evergreen bush
The tinkle, tinkle sound.

There it boasts…
The splendidness of light
The beauty of its being
The impression 'all is right'
The gifts beneath all perfect
The chocolates on the tree
The crackers lay awaiting for their eventuality.

There it stood…
Long ago, that other tree,
No baubles, tinsel, pretty lights
Just a cross of misery
Two trees though poles apart
With Christ though a part of each
Don't leave Christ out of your Christmas
Or you'll leave Him out of reach.

There it is…
For those who'll understand
The Gift from God on that tree
And the life for you He's planned
His gift's not tinsel wrapped
But the light will never fade
His gift is your salvation
And the price already paid.

Jackie Doherty.

21st December

WISE MEN... STILL SEEK HIM.

22nd December

I wonder, dear reader, if it's the same in your household?

Do you pack away all the Christmas lights each year wondering if they'll be okay for the next Christmas? Last year we purchased some new lights, some LED ones and so we had a redundant set of lights, which I put to one side to check at a future time. (it takes me such a long time to dress the tree these days!) That evening I couldn't sleep and got up to make a warm drink and saw the said, old lights, laying limp and rather useless, ready to be tested.

As I began unravelling them and before I could plug them in, I had a thought about how much like those lights we are, unless we are actually plugged into the main (!! Don't try this at home, it is an analogy!!) the main, that is the power of God, then we remain limp and rather useless.

As soon as we 'plug' into that divine power, we become bright lights that can shine in the darkness.

Are you plugged in?

23rd December

Many years ago now, almost twenty to be exact, I was preparing the Sunday school, to perform the annual nativity for the congregation and had hoped to include every child in some way and so some weeks before, made an appeal for the children to attend rehearsals, explaining that there were still some parts not yet filled for the various scenes, we needed sheep, cattle, and a Christmas Robin, with that, the hand of a little boy shot up with such enthusiasm, he had started attending church but didn't yet come to Sunday school, he told me later that he wanted to be the Christmas robin, not wanting to lose him, I assured him the role was his. I asked if he had a costume and he immediately said he did.

Imagine my surprise at rehearsal when he turned up with a gun, a neckerchief over his face, a booty bag swung over his back and was dressed in black!

I was very tactful when I asked him to remind me which part he'd been given to which he replied: 'I'm the Christmas robber.'

You and I know, that there is hardly a place in the nativity for a Christmas robin, but there is definitely NO place for a Christmas robber!!

24th December

'Christmas is not a time or a season but a state of mind. To cherish Peace and Goodwill, to be plenteous in mercy, is to have the real spirit of Christmas. If we think on these things, there will be born in us a saviour and over us will shine a star sending its gleam of hope to the world.'

Calvin Coolidge (1872 - 1933)

Presidential message 25/12/1927

25th December

This very day, all over the world there will be the giving and receiving of presents between family members, friends, neighbours, in homes of all types from palaces to tenement buildings.

Often these gifts will be given for all the wrong reasons, given grudgingly, mostly the gifts will never last!

For most of us it's difficult to remember what gifts we received the Christmas before! (I often use this exercise in helping people when they have difficulty sleeping! After all the usual things of breathing deeply, a warm drink, listening to relaxing music, lavender smellies etc, I then encourage them to do a little exercise of going back two years to Christmas, and tell them to try to recall each present they received... it usually works every time... they drop off to sleep!)

Although God gives us many gifts indeed, I believe that our lives are a 'gift' from God, and that what we do with them is our 'gift' to Him. The Holy Spirit is a 'gift', our children are 'gifts' and then of course there are different 'gifts' for different people, but at Christmas time, it is a time to reflect on the 'gift' God gives to each of us in the 'present' of His Son. Many people today will open every present they receive, it would be rude to not open a gift that had been chosen and bought at a price for us, and yet that is what many do, they leave the best present of all 'unopened' and 'disregarded' sometimes not even knowing of 'its' existence. This Christmas for those of us who know of this most wonderful 'gift' let it be a day, when we can share the true Christmas message with someone who has never heard it.

This is the greatest gift that we can ever give anyone.

Girl: "Mummy, will daddy be surprised by the present you've bought him this Christmas?"

Mother: "Yes, dear!" He was expecting a Porsche!"

Ok! You'll need your thinking caps!!

QUIZ

Christmas Morning: David, Fred and George have all received a gift, from the following information can you work out who got what.

1. David will not get the socks unless Fred gets the tie.

2. David will not get the cigars unless George gets the socks.

3. David will not get the tie unless Fred gets the cigars.

4. George will not get the socks unless David gets the tie

5. Fred will not get the cigars unless George gets the tie.

Answers overleaf...

26th December

"Teacher, which is the greatest commandment in the Law?"

Jesus replied: " 'Love the Lord your God with all your heart and with all your soul and with all your mind.'

This is the first and greatest commandment.

And the second is like it: 'Love your neighbour as yourself.'

All the Law and the Prophets hang on these two commandments.'"

Jesus speaking, in Matthew 22:36-40.

27th December

IT'S TIME

It's time dear friends to say farewell.
And to offer you thanks for being 'here'
To pray that God will Bless us all
As now we face a new 'New Year'.

No eye has seen, no ear has heard
Nor mind conceived what lays ahead
But we're assured of our Father's care
And cast our cares on Him instead.

With reverence and with grateful heart
Let's count our blessings one by one
And offer thanks and praise indeed
To Father, Spirit and precious Son.

Jackie Doherty.

28th December

(Answers to Quiz: David got the socks. George got the cigars. Fred got the tie.)

....

29th December

Here we are at the end of the year, dear readers, and I would like to thank you if you have 'stayed' with me to the end!

It has been a real pleasure for me to recall some old jokes, share stories and some of my poems with you in this way. I have prayed earnestly that each reader, (believer or not) would be encouraged by this book to go deeper into the things of God - to seek for yourself, wisdom; to pursue the gifts that God has in store for you. May you know that you are loved with a passion just as you are and understand that there is nothing you can do to make God love you any more, likewise there is nothing you can do to make God love you any less!

He loves you, as you are!

That doesn't mean to say that He will leave you as you are!! Not at all, He wants the very best for you.

As we approach 2011, not one of us knows what lies ahead for each of us, but we can trust our future to God, the good times and the bad! God never promises us an easy life... but He promises to be with us... every step of the way!

30th December

I just couldn't close dear friend, without taking this opportunity of wishing you all a very Happy and Blessed year ahead.

For those readers who may not yet have a personal relationship with God, then now, today, as we move towards a New Year may be just the right time to seek Him. You may wonder how on earth you begin, you may feel childish (this is a great start, because Jesus himself says "I tell you the truth, anyone who will not receive the kingdom of God like a little child will never enter it" Mark 10:15...).

May I say that already, God knows your heart and will respond to your seeking!

Before you close this page, if you are earnestly seeking, then I would say to you, close your eyes and call upon His name and pray in your own clumsy (I believe God isn't bothered about eloquent prayers, just heartfelt ones) words, something... along the lines of:

> *Father God, Jesus, Holy Spirit,*
> *I come to you now, just as I am.*
> *You know me and all that I am.*
> *I believe that Jesus is the Son of God*
> *and that He died for my sins.*
> *I confess all of my sin,*
> *known and unknown before You.*
> *I repent of all my sin.*
> *I trust you for my future.*
> *I invite you into my heart now.*
> *Father God, I believe... help me with my unbelief.*

When you pray along these lines you can believe that God has heard your cry. Everyone's experience is different you may feel wonderful, you may cry, you may wonder has He heard and want to pray it again, be assured He has heard and your life will take on new meaning for evermore!

If you have just prayed a similar prayer, before closing this book then I would say to you Shalom! dear fellow believer, welcome to the Christian walk, you really should now find another believer/ minister/ friend and share what you have just prayed. Get yourself a Bible and start living as God intended. Jesus said:

"Come to me, all who are weary and burdened and I will give you rest." Matthew 11:28

'Seek the Lord while He may be found; call on Him while He is near.' Isaiah 55:6.

'I have come that they may have life, and have it to the full.' Jesus speaking in John 11:10b.

'Come near to God and He will come near to you.' James 4:8.

....

31st December

Every good wish indeed to you, whatever your faith, have a wonderful year ahead.

The best is yet to come!

Jackie
x